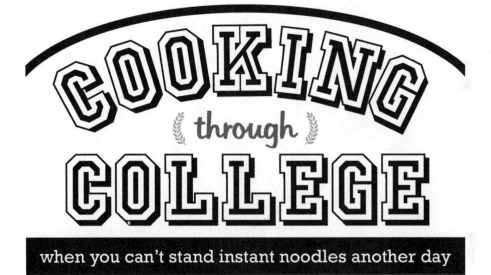

COOKING through COLLEGE

when you can't stand instant noodles another day

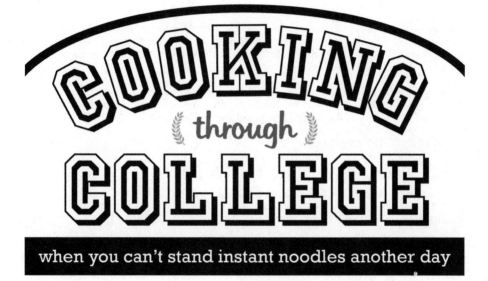

COOKING *through* COLLEGE

when you can't stand instant noodles another day

Chelsea Jackson
&
A. N. Gephart

Front Table Books
An imprint of Cedar Fort, Inc.
Springville, Utah

ISBN 13: 978-1-4621-1866-3

Published by Front Table Books, an imprint of Cedar Fort, Inc.
2373 W. 700 S., Springville, UT 84663
Distributed by Cedar Fort, Inc., www.cedarfort.com

LIBRARY OF CONGRESS CATALOGING-IN-PUBLICATION DATA

Names: Jackson, Chelsea, 1989- | Gephart, A. N. (Ashley N.), 1990-
Title: Cooking through college / Chelsea Jackson and A.N. Gephart.
Description: Springville, Utah : Front Table Books, an imprint of Cedar Fort, Inc., [2016] | Includes index.
Identifiers: LCCN 2016023572 (print) | LCCN 2016024536 (ebook) | ISBN 9781462118663 (perfect bound : acid-free paper) | ISBN 9781462126583 (epub, pdf, mobi)
Subjects: LCSH: Cooking. | College students--Life skills guides. | LCGFT: Cookbooks.
Classification: LCC TX714 .J315 2016 (print) | LCC TX714 (ebook) | DDC 641.5--dc23
LC record available at https://lccn.loc.gov/2016023572

Cover design by M. Shaun McMurdie
Cover design © 2016 by Cedar Fort, Inc.
Edited and typeset by Justin Greer

Printed in the United States of America

10 9 8 7 6 5 4 3 2

Printed on acid-free paper

PRAISE FOR *COOKING THROUGH COLLEGE* AND THE AUTHORS

"Any young person learning to cook for themselves will love *Cooking Through College*! I definitely wish I'd had this book when I was in school, and my husband and I have loved using it as a newly married couple! The recipes are easy to follow, don't require a lot of preparation time, and are absolutely delicious. The authors do a great job providing tips and tricks for how to store the leftovers as well as how to adjust each recipe to meet different dietary restrictions. There's so much variety in the recipes of this book; you won't be disappointed!"
—Rhiannon Cameron, University of Utah graduate

"Because of this book, there's really no excuse to go without nutritious, delicious, and affordable homemade meal options. Especially as newlyweds, we're constantly looking for healthier, cheaper alternatives to eating out. This book has saved us from more than one potential 'hangry' occasion. It's a must have!"
—McKenzie and Henry Unga of Bravelittlelungs.com

"Chelsea Jackson has written a fun and inviting cookbook for a new and energetic population, our students. She fills this crucial need with much understanding as it was not long ago when she was a student herself. She, too, lived a very hectic lifestyle as she juggled homework, roommates, a little sleep, fast meals, social life and whatever else she could fit in her crazy schedule. She realized early in her schooling how important healthier, sustainable, and quick and easy meals would make her feel, while also bringing comfort to her budget.

For the last year, Chelsea has been compiling a cookbook

filled with mouth-watering recipes and healthy options that are both delicious and satiating (or satisfying). This cookbook is full of awesome ideas, tips, tools, and all of the right elements to help a college student succeed on a fixed budget. Students will also experience delicious meals with many healthy alternatives in mind. Chelsea has involved all groups, even those with food sensitivities, so whether you have gluten or dairy issues or no food sensitivities, this cookbook is for you. Her contagious voice is heard throughout to keep you entertained and wanting more. Enjoy these pages that are filled with yumminess and love and can be enjoyed by all!"
—Trisha Jamison, Health and Wellness Coach, ACE fitness instructor, and owner of JamisonWellness

"My favorite is the Italian stuffed bell peppers! They are seriously divine! But you can't go wrong with any of these recipes. They are fantastic!"
—Alyssa Smith, wife of a student attending Eastern Washington University

"Chelsea and Ashley are really on to something! Having taken care of college age young adults for many years, [I know that] students need an alternative to the way they eat. There is no excuse for the 'freshman 20' that so many students add to their waistlines. They have put together meals and snacks that are easy, fun, tasty, and certainly healthier than the foods college students would otherwise choose. Ideal for the student who is experiencing their first time away from mommy's kitchen, or even one who is tired of the same old poor food choices, *Cooking Though College* will have something for every taste and gives alternatives for people with food sensitivities. Since gluten intolerance is on the rise, having that option is especially useful, and there are SO MANY options. No need to eat boring food. Not with *Cooking Through College*! It reads

like a comic book and will make a party in your mouth!"
—Jeffrey R. Jamison, DO, FAAFP

"I was sold on this before the first recipe even started. With helpful tips on grocery shopping on a budget, which spices to keep on hand, and how to make your recipes low-fat or gluten-free, there is something here for everyone. Make sure you try the Peanut Butter Banana Shake, Mongolian Beef, or Thai Chicken Coconut Soup. These easy recipes don't make you compromise on taste, health, or variety. I wish I would have had this when I was in college."
—Emily Chambers, author of *The Cheese Lover's Cookbook*

Contents

Contents

Contents

INTRODUCTION

Let's be straight here, college students don't have time to sleep—let alone cook. Unless meals magically pop out of this cookbook, what guarantees that this cookbook is crucial for every college student to have? Good food feeds the brain. Crappy food makes you feel like crap and think like crap. So it is time for you to make good food (both in taste and quality) a priority.

Don't go thinking you can just eat better food and then nail all your tests and ace all your classes. You still have to work, but like a well-cared-for car, you will run better with healthier food (and more sleep).

These recipes are designed around short cook times, prepare-and-leave slow cooker meals, or make-ahead foods. The idea is to cook more food less often so that you have time to tackle all your responsibilities without forfeiting your health by eating frozen burritos and fast food. Plus, food is going to be around your whole life. You might as well learn how to make it well. Whether you are a guy or girl, knowing how to cook is high on many peoples' "must-have" lists for potential suitors. Impress them and learn how to cook.

This book will be a great tutor for you as you start your own cooking journey. The recipes are written simply so anyone can follow them. We have carefully selected and perfected 150 recipes that will help you save money, teach you to cook, and help your brain and body work right.

Watch for these icons:

GLUTEN-FREE!—Because it's a thing. A majority of our recipes have a gluten-free alternative. All of Chelsea Jackson's recipes were originally made gluten-free.

DAIRY-FREE! or **COW-FREE!**—Also a thing. Many of Ashley Gephart's recipes are dairy-free, have dairy-free alternatives, or use goat and sheep dairy.

SPICY!—Who doesn't love a kick of spice once in awhile? Or all the time? The pepper levels range from a little kick (1 pepper) to super spicy (3 peppers)!

◎ LEFTOVERS!—This is the main objective of this book—to make leftovers so you cook less often but have great leftover meals already prepared for you to grab and go. And sometimes you just need leftovers or bigger meals to feed your roommates, or a date, or because you are just really hungry after studying in the library all day . . .

❄ FREEZE!—Many of our recipes can be easily frozen. We recommend you divide out your dinner or lunch amounts in Ziplock baggies and freeze them. That way you can control your portion size as well as have a quick meal to toss in the microwave and eat within minutes.

⏱ FAST!—Sometimes you only have a short amount of time to make something edible for yourself. Look for this icon when you are having one of those days.

Ⓔ EASY!—All of these recipes are easy, but some of them are SUPER easy and taste way more impressive than your skills or energy should allow.

⊘ HEALTHY!—These recipes are all intended to be healthy, though we do throw in quite a few that are exceptionally healthy and a few fun ones that may not be as healthy.

Besides the more detailed tips found towards the end of this introduction, you will be able to find Time-Saving Tips, Money-Saving Tips, Health Tips, and Cooking Tips throughout the book.

Time-Saving Tips

College students are notorious for running by the seat of their pants. They pack so much stuff in their days that they don't have time to think about it, let alone plan for it, just go, go, go. Each day turns into a race and almost a competition to see how much can be packed in and how fast it can get done. Here are a couple of tips to help you keep yourself full and happy.

Get the right tools

You don't HAVE to have all these devices to use this book, though some things like pots or pans are essential. We have found some of the following things helpful to save on time and increase the quality and taste of your food.

Normally your local Walmart or even Target may have affordable cooking tools. We recommend that you look up the products you are investigating online (Amazon works great) to see their ratings, especially for

Crock-Pots and rice cookers. You may also find a steal of a deal at local secondhand stores in your area. You might also check Craigslist.com to see if anyone in your area is trying to get rid of some of the following items:

- Rice cooker
- Crock-Pot
- Basic pan set (large pot and large pan, preferably the nonstick kind)
- Sharp knives (If they turn a tomato into tomato sauce, you need new ones.)
- Rubber spatula, used for baking
- Blender
- Hand mixer
- Wooden spoon: These won't get hot over a stove, and they are great for those super-hot recipes like candy that could melt plastic and destroy your food. They do burn over too much heat, though, so do not leave them sitting in a pot.

Plan ahead

If you plan what you want to eat for the week, you will save not only time but also a significant amount of money. Plan the meals you will make during the week before you go to the grocery store. It is also important to consider your schedule. If you have some days that are just crazy busy and other days that are a bit slower, plan to make food on your slower days and enjoy the leftovers on your crazy days. Make a grocery list based off what you need for the week. One trip to the grocery store will save you a lot of time and money.

Also, at the end of this cookbook on page 231 you will find an index of unique ingredients that we use throughout the book. If you have extra of some of these ingredients, consider making another recipe that requests that ingredient so you don't waste food.

Save time at the grocery store

When you make your list, organize your items in categories according to the layout of the grocery store so you don't ping-pong around trying to get everything you need. That will only increase the amount of time you spend there, your frustration, and the likelihood that you will miss something and waste time going back later in the week.

Here are some categories to use:

- Produce

- Dairy/cheese
- Meat
- Frozen foods
- Baking (spices are normally down this aisle)
- Pasta or Hispanic food
- Cans (from fruits to soups)

Make bigger meals and embrace the leftovers

You know your schedule better than anyone. Make sure you plan your meals around what you can do and what you need. Make bigger meals when you have a little extra time. Sometimes that might be on the weekend. Look for recipes that have the Leftover icon, so you can have food ready during your busy (or sometimes lazy) days. But if you make bigger meals, you will spend less time cooking overall.

Save dry mixes for those busy times

Make dry mixes for a rainy day, like pancake mix (page 14), or take the base dry ingredients from a recipe and store in an airtight, resealable bag until you need to use it. Keep track of the date you've stored it, since it will not last forever.

Money-Saving Tips

Just because you are short on funds doesn't mean you should eat crappy food. Here are a couple things to do to make eating healthy easier (in the long term) on your budget.

Allot one trip a week to the grocery store with a list in hand

If you put in the time to make a grocery list and only go once a week to the grocery store, you will save money and be able to plan out your budget better. It is important that you already know how much you can spend at the store each week. Sometimes it helps people to take a set amount of cash and only spend that much money. If you make homemade food and avoid fast food (although an occasional trip isn't against the law), you will make your body and your budget feel better.

Buy the things you use often in greater quantity

Learn what you like and eat a lot of. It might be worth the effort to buy those things in greater quantities. One suggestion would be to buy a large bag of frozen chicken. Chicken is pretty cheap and can be used for many different recipes within this cookbook.

Other items you may want to have on hand include oil, bouillon, lemon juice, spices, and herbs.

Many ingredients in this book, like fish sauce, can be used between multiple recipes in different amounts, so you don't need to buy a bottle of something obscure that you'll use only a few times before it goes bad. Take note of these, and plan your shopping list and meal plan around them to save yourself money.

Don't go to the grocery store while you are hungry

If you go to the grocery store while you are starving, your impulsive monkey brain will take over. All of a sudden you will find your cart heaped with donuts, frozen pizzas, and chips with nearly no nutritional value. This will not help you do better in school, eat healthier, or save money. Don't go to the store hungry. Have a plan and stick to it.

Believe in coupons

If you have the time to spare, like during a movie you've already seen five times or your Netflix binge, make the effort to clip coupons out of your newspaper or find them online. Yes, you may look like that lady at the grocery store with five hundred coupons who holds up the line and brings a weary look to the cashier's face. But those dollars and cents will add up quickly, particularly with brand foods or meat, and your wallet will thank you. It also may help with buying special ingredients for a fancy meal.

Grow an herb garden

Make the effort to grow your own herbs. Your recipes will taste better all around, and you'll have the added benefit of knowing where some of your ingredients come from. Do your research to learn how to keep them alive.

Keep track of your food

Use a magnetic notepad on your fridge and freezer to keep track of when you buy meats and vegetables, or when you make a meal that has leftovers. Make sure all your roommates use it as well. That way, you know when you have leftovers, or when you have an ingredient you need to use. You'll save yourself the sorrow of throwing out food you haven't used! You'll also spare yourself (and your nose) the agony of opening the fridge in the morning, and the subsequent hunt for the guilty Tupperware container in the back of the shelf.

Health Tips

Here are some fantastic health tips you can implement into your diet that will make a difference in how you feel and think. Your body craves good healthy food, not just good-tasting food. Unfortunately, most of the time, the cheapest route isn't the healthiest route. However, there are some adjustments you can make that will make a tremendous difference.

Focus on produce

Your cart should be predominantly full of fresh produce. College students often forget how important vegetables and fruit are when their moms are no longer cooking for them. Say no to scurvy.

Limit your cheese and creams

Most people love LOTS of cheese but being moderate with this ingredient will help you stay fit and healthy. Some of our recipes include delicious creamy concoctions, but if you want to avoid the heavy cream and its lovely calories and fat, use evaporated skim milk or other options listed in the individual recipes. Ricotta cheese is also a healthier alternative to cream cheese.

Why goat and sheep dairy?

Milk allergies and lactose intolerance are becoming more and more prevalent in today's food-sensitive world. While it does not work for everyone with certain intolerances and allergies, goat and sheep dairy can provide alternatives to cow dairy products. The proteins in these milks breaks down much more easily than cow milk, which has thicker fat globules and more lactose in general. The stronger taste may take some getting used to, but the benefits of cow-free dairy are worth it!

Avoid white breads

Try to avoid white breads because the flour has been bleached and essentially stripped away of many of the nutrients that even make it useful. Grains will fill you with the good stuff that your body needs to operate at the best of its ability.

Not all meats are created equal

This cookbook uses a range of different types of meat, but as a general rule, know that packaged meats are full of preservatives that your body does not want. This includes lunch meats, sausage, hotdogs, and pepperoni. If you are looking for healthier options, trade these meats for ground turkey, chicken, hamburger, or chicken sausage. Also, check the ingredient lists on the packages of packed meats. If there are lots of chemicals listed, avoid that package.

Keep to frozen foods

Buy frozen foods instead of canned foods whenever possible. They are healthier because they have fewer preservatives and are normally picked (for fruit or vegetables) when they were more ripe.

If you can't say it, don't buy it

Pay attention to the ingredient lists on packaged food and cans. If you can't pronounce the ingredients, try to avoid that specific option. The extra chemicals and preservatives are not good for you. There are other packaged, canned, or jarred options that have shorter ingredients lists that you can pronounce.

Oils

There are lots of different cooking oil options you can use. Both of us normally use extra virgin olive oil, avocado oil, or coconut oil. But when it comes to oil, remember that when it begins to smoke, you are actually breaking the bonds and turning it into trans fat—and you don't want that. Avocado oil has a higher heat tolerance, which makes it a wonderful companion in the kitchen. Coconut oil also has a higher heat tolerance, and the fat is converted directly into energy, which makes it much healthier for you.

Cooking Tips

Anyone can cook, but it takes practice to become a good cook. There are also different kinds of cooks: those who can't follow a recipe and love to be creative and experiment and those who are perfectly happy following every step in a recipe. The world needs both types of cooks. But in order to become the best cook you can be, we suggest the following tips.

Where to start

Read the recipe all the way through once. As you read, pull out the ingredients and tools you will need. If you do this, you'll be less likely to skip an ingredient or step, and you will have everything you need on hand, which makes things faster!

Be creative

If you are not very comfortable in the kitchen yet, we suggest that you follow the directions closely. But don't be afraid to be creative and explore new options and alterations to the recipes we have created for you. Many of these recipes included in this book had a base we started with and then we added our own unique changes. Have fun with cooking!

Discover some cooking secrets

There are a lot of cooking hacks you will discover the more you cook. Here are a few to give you a head start.

Brown sugar: Every time you measure brown sugar, unless the recipe specifically says otherwise, always pack it tightly into the measuring cup.

Powdered sugar: Always sift when adding to a recipe, even if it's a pain. This helps remove lumps from the sugar, and controls the amount spread over a dessert.

Room temperature eggs and butter: Unless a recipe says otherwise, eggs, butter, and often cream cheese should be added at room temperature. But what do you do if you forget to leave your eggs and butter out before cooking?

- **For butter**: Run a drinking glass under hot water until glass is very warm. Set a stick of butter on its end and stand the glass upside-down over it. By the time you're ready to use it, it will be room temperature!

- **For eggs**: Fill a dish with warm (but not boiling hot) water. Set egg carefully into the water. By the time you need to use it, it should be room temperature!

Breaking eggs: Always break eggs into a separate bowl from your mixing bowl. This will spare you stress if you drop shells into your mix, or worse—a bad egg. If you have to separate whites from yolks, use yet another bowl: one for breaking the current egg, one for the whites, and one for the yolks. That way, if yolk accidentally gets into your egg white, you won't have to start over completely.

To separate eggs, break the shell as neatly in half as possible. Gently slide yolk from shell to shell, and the white should slip out. Or, you can use a slotted spoon to let the egg white separate from the yolk. Do not let any yolk get into the whites. The protein in the yolks prevents the whites from getting fluffy when you beat them.

Bad eggs: Sell-by dates on the egg carton might not always be accurate, depending on how you store eggs and the temperature of your fridge. However, they may not always smell bad or show obvious signs of spoilage when they've reached their sell-by date. How do you tell if an egg is bad? Fill a drinking glass with water. Carefully lower the egg into the water and let go. If it floats, it's bad. If it sinks, it's good to use. If it hovers in the middle, you should use it as soon as possible.

Alternately, if you break open an egg, you can tell it's bad if the "umbilical cord" on the yolk has disappeared, and the yolk is runny.

Steak without a meat thermometer: Can't afford yet another kitchen gadget? There's an easy way to test the doneness of steak without a meat thermometer. First, make a circle with your finger and thumb. Press on the muscle just below and to the side of your thumb. That's what rare steak should feel like when you press on it! Repeat with each finger:

Middle finger and thumb: Medium

Ring finger and thumb: Medium-well

Pinky finger and thumb: Well-done

Thawing chicken: There are several ways to thaw out your chicken.

1. Put the amount of frozen chicken you need in a covered bowl in your fridge overnight.

2. Thaw your chicken in the microwave, but make sure to submerge it in water. This will prevent your chicken from drying out. Remember, you don't want to cook your chicken in the microwave, just thaw it out.

    While you can thaw frozen chicken in the microwave, these appliances target the water in food, which may give an unpleasant taste to chicken, even after it's been seasoned and cooked. If you have don't have time to leave it in the refrigerator overnight, but want to save your taste buds, try this:

3. Make sure chicken is in an airtight, resealable bag. Fill a large bowl with hot water from the sink, and place chicken in the water. Check on it every 15 minutes or so, turning it in the water because some ends will stick out. If necessary, throw out the water when it gets cold and replace with more hot water. Chicken will be ready when there is no

more ice visible and the chicken is squishy to the touch.

Cornstarch: If you're making a recipe that normally uses a little flour, like in a roux, but you need it to be gluten-free, use cornstarch. Use half of what you would for flour, as cornstarch thickens better than most all-purpose wheat flour. You can also use arrowroot or potato flakes, but watch out for trans fats with potato flakes! You don't want those!

Measuring: Use the back of a knife to sweep excess flour, sugar, etc. back into the package and get the most accurate measurement possible. It also helps save that ingredient for future use!

Onions: It's important to manage the sting of slicing onions, especially if you're making food for guests and don't want to look like you just wept your way through a Hallmark movie. There are two great ways: soak the onion in a bowl of cold water for 15 minutes before you need it; or, if you forgot or need a stronger onion, put a piece of bread in your mouth while you're slicing.

Definitions of Cooking Methods:

Some of the words we use in our recipes may be unfamiliar to you, so here is a guide.

- **Chop**: To slice into large or bite-size pieces.

- **Crush:** To get the smallest possible pieces out of an ingredient by using a rolling pin or mortar and pestle.

- **Dice**: To slice into smaller pieces than chopping. Often refers to cutting into cubes.

- **Mince**: To slice into very tiny pieces, as small as you can get, that spread well through the recipe and are not overwhelming to bite into.

- **Julienne**: To slice into to thin piecies, about the size and width of a matchstick.

- **Boil**: To heat up liquid hot enough that it begins to bubble.

- **Rolling boil**: This is one step higher than just your typical boil. Water should be bubbling and churning.

- **Simmer**: To keep food cooking at a temperature just below boiling point.

- **Sauté**: To fry food, often onions or garlic, very quickly in a little bit of fat such as oil or butter.

- **Dredge**: To coat meat in flour or cornstarch and then brown in a pan. This gives the meat a nice texture that is highly desirable in many recipes.

- **Fold**: A gentle way to combine mixtures together, especially if one has to stay fluffy! Use a large bowl and as wide a spatula as you have, and work with a scoop and fold motion, turning the bowl as you do so. Stirring, whisking, or beating will only damage your fluffy mixtures, so resist the urge! This technique does require patience, but you'll get the hang of it.

- **Cream**: In many baking recipes, you need to cream the butter and sugar together first thing. If you don't have a mixer, here's how to do it by hand. Add the sugar to the butter and gently mash them with a fork. Using a wooden spoon, stir until light and fluffy. Scrape the sides of the bowl with a rubber spatula every so often.

- **Heaping cup**: The cup should be overflowing with whatever ingredient the recipe calls for.

- **Combine vs. Mix**: Generally in cooking, you combine solids and mix liquids. The practice is the same where you stir the ingredients together.

Build Your Spice Stash

In order to truly be a pro in the kitchen, we recommend you begin building your spice stash. We use quite a few spices throughout our recipes. Here are a few we recommend you always keep on hand.

Salt
Pepper
Chili powder
Cumin
Basil
Oregano
Parsley
Rosemary
Italian Seasoning
Paprika
Curry Powder
Onion Powder
Garlic Powder
Red pepper flakes (if you like spicy food!

BREAKFAST

PANCAKE MIX

Save yourself a bit of money and stress by making pancake mix from scratch and storing it for those mornings when you need brain food, but have no time or money to devote to a grocery store trip or a greasy fast-food substitute.—Ashley

Makes 10 pancakes | Time: 10 minutes

1½ cups flour
3 tsp. baking powder
½ tsp. salt
1 Tbsp. sugar
1¼ cups milk
1 egg
3 Tbsp. butter, melted
1 tsp. vanilla

COOKING TIP:
This recipe doubles well! If you're making to save for later, it's roughly 1½ cup mix to wet ingredients (amounts listed above) per 10 pancakes.

1. Mix together dry ingredients. If saving for another time, store in a resealable, airtight bag.

2. When ready to use, blend in milk, egg, butter, and vanilla until smooth.

3. Heat griddle over medium heat and pour about ¼ cup batter onto griddle to form each pancake. Flip when bubbles are visible on the top, and cook till golden brown on both sides.

CHOCOLATE CHOCOLATE CHIP PANCAKES

These chocolate pancakes are quick and easy with the perfect amount of chocolatey sweetness to satisfy your morning sweet-tooth but not enough that it sends you into a sugar buzz all through your morning classes. You are welcome to use your favorite pancake mix or the pancake mix from the previous page.—Chelsea

Makes 6 pancakes | Time: 15 minutes

1 cup pancake mix
1 Tbsp. cocoa powder
1 egg
2 Tbsp. oil
1 tsp. vanilla
2 Tbsp. semi-sweet chocolate chips

Optional Toppings:
syrup
butter
peanut butter

1.   Mix all ingredients together using a metal whisk. If mix seems too thick, add a bit of water.

2.   Heat pan or skillet to medium heat. Butter pan and pour ¼ cup batter in pan. Cook until bubbles are visible on the top and then flip and cook for another 3 to 4 minutes.

3.   Add desired toppings and drizzle with hot syrup.

(with gluten-free
pancake mix)

STUFFED FRENCH TOAST

Make a special breakfast memorable with French toast that leaves you wondering why you don't have it every single morning! It's a bit more complicated than the normal variety, but as long as you have a sharp enough knife, it shouldn't take up too much more time.—Ashley

Makes 4–5 slices | Time: 10 minutes

French Toast:
4–5 slices of bread
3 eggs
2 tsp. cinnamon
3 Tbsp. milk
1 tsp. vanilla

> **TIME-SAVING TIP:**
> If you're in a rush, skip the stuffing and proceed directly to step 3.

Filling:
4 oz. cream cheese
2 tsp. vanilla
1½ tsp. lemon juice
1 tsp. lemon zest

1. Using a very sharp knife, slice a pocket in the top of each slice of bread, not cutting all the way through the sides or the bottom.

2. Combine filling ingredients and mix until smooth. Spread about 2 tablespoons. filling into each pocket and press closed.

3. Crack eggs in a sandwich-sized container (a pie pan works great too). Add cinnamon, milk, and vanilla and whisk together.

4. Place a pan on medium heat and coat with butter or coconut oil. Dip both sides of bread in egg mixture and place on skillet. Cook each side for around 4 minutes or until lightly browned.

Top with Buttermilk Syrup (following page), whipped cream, and strawberries, if desired.

BUTTERMILK SYRUP

This sweet, light, caramel-y syrup adds an excellent touch to cream cheese–based breakfasts or to fluffy pancakes. It practically turns breakfast into dessert!—Ashley

Makes 1½ cups syrup | Time: 10 minutes

1½ cups sugar
¾ cup buttermilk
½ cup butter
1 tsp. baking soda
2 tsp. vanilla

MONEY-SAVING TIP:
Don't have buttermilk? Stir 1 tablespoon lemon juice or vinegar into just under a cup of milk. Let stand for about 5 minutes before using.

HEALTH TIP:
For a healthier syrup alternative, avoid using syrup with high fructose corn syrup in it.

1. Heat sugar, buttermilk, and butter in a saucepan over medium heat until mixture begins to boil. Remove from heat and mix in baking soda and vanilla. Serve as soon as possible over breakfast.

EGG MUFFINS

Pop these healthy, quick-to-eat muffins in the microwave to eat before you run off to class or freeze them for later. With 12 muffins, this recipe could provide breakfast for nearly the whole week! Use a spoonful of salsa as an optional topping.—Chelsea

Makes 12 muffins | Time: 50 minutes

Crust
1 Tbsp. yeast
2 tsp. brown sugar
¾ cup very warm water (95–115 degrees)
1½–2 cups flour
1 egg
1 tsp. salt
3 Tbsp. coconut oil (melted) or other vegetable oil (recommend avocado)

Egg filling
½ lb. ground sausage
6 eggs
¼ cup milk
¼ cup chopped mushrooms
¼ cup chopped onions
¼ cup chopped green bell pepper
¼ cup chopped zucchini
1 cup shredded cheddar cheese

1. Preheat oven to 350 degrees.
2. Add yeast, brown sugar, and water in a small bowl. Let bowl sit for 5 minutes.
3. Add flour, egg, salt, oil, and yeast mixture into another bowl. Knead with hands until well mixed. Add flour as needed so dough doesn't stick to hands. Set aside.
4. Brown sausage in a pan. Then mix sausage in a bowl with eggs, milk, mushrooms, onions, bell pepper, and zucchini.

5. Oil a muffin pan. Break up dough into 12 balls. Pat each ball into a flat circle just a little bigger than your palm. Mold one into each cup.

6. Fill each up with egg filling and cover top with cheese.

7. Bake for about 18 minutes or until egg looks well cooked.

(without cheese)   (with gluten-
                                                              free flour)

ITALIAN PEPPERONI EGGS

Here is a better alternative to having pizza for breakfast!—Chelsea

Makes 4 open-faced sandwiches | Time: 10 minutes

6 eggs
¼ cup milk
10–15 slices pepperoni
4 slices bread
½ cup marinara sauce, heated
shredded mozzarella or cheddar cheese for topping

1. Mix eggs and milk in bowl.

2. Oil pan and cook eggs and pepperoni slices on medium-high heat for about 4 minutes or until cooked.

3. Toast bread and smear hot marinara sauce on one side of each slice. Divide eggs evenly between each slice with a sprinkle of cheese on top.

(with gluten-
free bread)

(without cheese and
with almond milk)

BREAKFAST PIZZA

This is a fun breakfast to make with friends or have leftovers for days. Hope you like hash browns! —Chelsea

Makes 8 slices | Time: 50 minutes

1 Tbsp. butter or oil (more if using a stoneware pizza pan)
1 (20-oz.) bag shredded hash browns, thawed
salt and pepper to taste
½ lb. ground sausage
4 eggs
2 Tbsp. milk
½ cup onions, diced
½ can Mexican stewed tomatoes, diced
1 cup green bell peppers, diced
½ cup mushrooms, sliced
½ cup zucchini or yellow squash, diced
2 cups shredded cheese
salsa and sour cream/Mexican table cream, optional

1. Preheat oven to 425 degrees.
2. Oil or butter cookie sheet or pizza pan. Spread out hash browns on pan and mold into pizza shape. Sprinkle with salt and black pepper.
3. Bake for 20 minutes.
4. Brown ground sausage in pan and place in another bowl. Crack 4 eggs and add 2 tablespoons of milk into separate bowl. Mix well then pour egg mixture into pan and scramble.
5. Once the oven timer goes off, spread sausage and scrambled eggs on hash brown crust.
6. Mix all diced and chopped veggies into a bowl with Mexican stewed tomatoes (with juices). Spread mixture over crust.
7. Bake for 10 minutes.
8. Pull pan out and sprinkle two cups of shredded cheese over top. Bake for another 10 minutes.
9. Slice like a pizza and add salsa or sour cream.

(cut all dairy products: milk, cheese, and sour cream)

MEXICAN PEPPER EGGS

Tired of eating the same style of eggs? Shake it up with these fun bell pepper–ringed eggs smothered in salsa.—Chelsea

Makes 4 eggs | Time: 10 minutes

1 green, red, or yellow bell pepper (Cooking Tip: Red, yellow, or orange bell peppers add a sweeter flavor.)
1 Tbsp. oil
4 eggs
½–1 cup shredded cheese
4–6 Tbsp. salsa
crema or sour cream to drizzle, optional

> *Mexican table cream or "crema" is a wonderful alternative to sour cream. It is not as sour and more creamy.*

1. Cut bell pepper in about ½-inch thick rings with seeds and centers removed.
2. In a medium pan, add oil and bell pepper rings on medium/high heat. Slowly crack an egg into the center of each pepper ring so egg doesn't leak out and yolk doesn't break.
3. Cover pan and cook for 2½–3 minutes. Carefully flip each egg over and cook for 1 minute. (If you don't like a runny yolk then cook for an additional 2½–3 minutes.) Then sprinkle cheese on top.
4. Place on a plate with salsa and sour cream or crema.

(without cheese or crema/ sour cream)

CROCK-POT HASH BROWN CASSEROLE

This is a fun breakfast to make for dinner and use the leftovers in the morning! You are guaranteed to hum in pleasure at the delicious creamy taste.—Chelsea

Makes 4–5 servings | Time: 2½–3 hours

1 lb. ground sausage
3 Tbsp. butter
1 cup chopped mushrooms
1 cup chopped onion
1 cup chopped green bell pepper
¼ tsp. garlic powder
3 Tbsp. flour
1 cup milk
½ cup sour cream
1 cup shredded Colby Jack or cheddar cheese
2 Tbsp. dried parsley
½ tsp. black pepper
½ tsp. salt
1 (26-oz.) package frozen shredded hash browns

1. Cook ground sausage on medium heat until browned. Set aside.

2. Heat butter in a pan on medium and then add mushrooms, onions, and bell peppers. Sauté veggies until soft. Add in garlic powder, flour, and milk. Mix on low heat until thickened.

3. Take pan off heat and add sour cream, cheese, parsley, salt, and pepper.

4. Mix sausage, hash browns, and creamy mixture together in a Crock-Pot. Turn Crock-Pot on high for 2½–3 hours.

5. Thirty minutes before you eat, uncover Crock-Pot and continue cooking so the top can get a bit crispy. Add more cheese and parsley to the top if desired.

(with gluten-free flour)

BREAKFAST SAUSAGE TAQUITOS

Use these leftovers as a quick breakfast the next day that you can warm up in the microwave before having to run out the door.—Chelsea

Makes 14 taquitos | Time: 30–35 minutes

½ lb. pork sausage
6 eggs
¼ cup milk
⅓ cup diced onion
⅓ cup diced red bell pepper
¼ cup diced tomato
½ cup cheddar cheese
2 Tbsp. feta cheese (optional but super yummy!)
2½ Tbsp. oil
1 cup chopped spinach
14 corn tortillas

Optional Toppings:
avocado slices
salsa
crema or sour cream

1. Preheat oven to 425 degrees.
2. Brown sausage in a medium pan. Set aside.
3. Mix eggs, milk, onion, red pepper, tomato, cheddar cheese, and feta cheese in a bowl. Heat a pan with oil on medium heat. Add egg mixture and spinach. Stir frequently until cooked.
4. Wrap corn tortillas in a damp towel and put in the microwave for 1–2 minutes so they are more pliable.
5. Oil a 9 x 13 pan. Fill each tortilla with 2–3 spoonfuls of egg mixture, roll tortilla, and then place it in pan,

seam-side down. Dampen a paper towel with oil and wipe prepared tortilla tops.

6. Bake for 15–20 minutes or until golden.

7. Top taquitos with avocado, salsa, and crema/sour cream.

(without cheese or crema/
sour cream)

BREAKFAST BURRITO

This recipe comes from my friend Hannah Dunaway. If you make the bacon and potatoes the night before, all you have to do is zap the ingredients in a microwave, wrap them in a tortilla, and take it to go.—Ashley

Makes 1 burrito | Time: 15 minutes
(or 5 minutes if made ahead)

2 large potatoes OR 3 small potatoes
1 tsp. olive oil
6 strips bacon, fried and crumbled
7 eggs, scrambled
salsa
sour cream
1 tortilla

1. Dice potatoes and fry in a skillet until soft. Remove from heat. This can be done ahead of time and the potatoes stored in an airtight container.

2. Mix potatoes with bacon and eggs. If made ahead, heat up in the microwave about 1 minute. Spoon into a tortilla. Top with salsa and sour cream to taste.

3. When tortilla is fully loaded, fold the top and bottom over the filling. Take the left side and fold it over the filling. Roll to the right, forming a neat burrito.

PEANUT BUTTER BANANA SHAKE

Need a quick, tasty, and healthy start to your day? Enjoy this creamy chocolate shake of goodness! It will make you feel full longer (thanks to the peanut butter!). Add more peanut butter or ice to thicken the shake.—Chelsea

Makes 2 glasses | Time: 8 minutes

2 frozen bananas, chopped
2 Tbsp. cocoa powder
1 cup milk or almond milk
¼ cup peanut butter
½ tsp. vanilla extract

1.   Place all ingredients in a blender and blend until smooth.

(with almond milk)

(add a handful of spinach for an extra dose of healthiness)

ORANGE SMOOTHIE

Smoothies are a great way to get energy in the morning on-the-go. However, it can be expensive to buy one every morning, no matter how much you love your favorite smoothie joint. Save yourself some cash by making your own!—Ashley

Makes 1 glass | Time: 2 minutes

¾ cup orange juice
¾ soy milk
1 scoop lime sherbet, to taste
1 scoop frozen yogurt
ice, to taste
whey or protein powder of choice, optional

1. Place all ingredients in a blender and pulse to break up ice. Then puree until smooth and serve immediately.

Variation: Add lemonade rather than orange juice for a tart and tangy drink.
If you have access to mango juice, give that a shot! For an extra kick, throw in a dash of chili powder. It's surprisingly amazing!

(with goat milk yogurt)

KEY LIME SHAKE

You can make this shake in the morning with a dash of whey or protein boost to get you started for your day, or you can serve just as seen below for a creamy, tart dinner drink.—Ashley

Makes 1 serving | Time: 2 minutes

2 Tbsp. margarita mixer
¼ cup orange juice
1 scoop vanilla ice cream
ice

1. Add all ingredients to a blender and blend until slushy. Serve immediately.

Variation: For a breakfast shake, add a scoop of your whey or protein boost of choice as you're adding ingredients to the blender.

FRUIT BREAKFAST SHAKE

Start your day with a tropical fruit shake to calm your nerves and give you the boost of energy you will need to tackle your day.—Chelsea

Makes 2 glasses | Time: 8 minutes

1 cup frozen fruit
I recommend tropical varieties
1 cup (or 6–8 oz.) vanilla yogurt
1 banana (preferably frozen)
1 cup milk or almond milk
1 handful of spinach leaves
1 tsp. chia seeds, optional

HEALTH TIP:
Chia seeds are one of the healthiest foods on the planet. They are full of antioxidants.

Place all ingredients in a blender. (If your banana is frozen, break it up into chunks for easy blending.) Blend together. Add a few ice cubes for a thicker shake.

CREAMY BANANA APPLE OATMEAL

Here is a hearty start to your day that will keep you plenty full until lunch!—Chelsea

Makes 2 bowls | Time: 15–20 minutes

1 cup uncooked oatmeal
¼ cup milk or almond milk
⅓ cup vanilla coffee creamer
¼ cup diced banana
¼ cup diced apple
Sprinkle of cinnamon
extra brown sugar or honey to sweeten, optional

> **HEALTH TIP:**
> If you want to avoid the coffee creamer, add about a tablespoon of honey instead.

1. Cook oatmeal by following directions on the package.

2. Once oatmeal is cooked, add milk, coffee creamer, banana, apple, and cinnamon to each bowl. Mix well and enjoy.

(depending on oatmeal)

(add a tablespoon of honey instead of coffee creamer to be healthier)

LUNCH

BEST BUTTER BURGER

Adding a little bit of fat back to the beef in the form of fresh butter makes these taste like the burgers from fast food joints, without the grease and done with considerably more flavor.—Ashley

Makes 4 burgers | Time: 15 minutes

2 lbs. ground beef
beef seasoning, or salt and pepper
1 Tbsp. Worcestershire sauce
1 egg
1 stick butter, softened
4 slices cheese
4 large burger buns

1. In a large bowl, mix beef, seasoning, Worcester-shire sauce, and egg until well-combined. If you use your hands, don't work it too long, or you will activate the fat in the beef and it will be lost during grilling.

2. Heat a grill or skillet. Slice the butter into thin patties, and form the beef into patties around 1–2 of them each. The butter will melt inside and help provide some flavor to the meat as it runs down. Sear the patties on both sides, and turn frequently until burgers are done through.

3. Removing patties from heat, top with a slice of cheese and serve on hamburger buns.

SUPREME NACHOS

Who wants wimpy nachos?!—Chelsea

Makes about 4 plates | Time: 15–20 minutes

1 lb. ground beef
1 taco seasoning packet
1 (16-oz.) can refried beans
1 (15.25-oz.) can corn
½ cup diced red onions
1–2 diced roma tomatoes
1 diced avocado
2 cups shredded cheese
1 bag corn tortilla chips
salsa and sour cream (or crema)

1. Brown ground beef in medium pan. Soak up grease with a paper towel and then follow instructions on taco seasoning packet.

2. Warm up beans on the stove and corn in the microwave.

3. Pile 2–3 handfuls of chips on a plate and add desired ingredients.

(without cheese and crema/sour cream)

PANINIS

Warm and flavorful, paninis are a great way to do grilled sandwiches and shake it up from the usual. You can also incorporate more greens onto a sandwich like this to make it healthier.—Ashley

Makes 4 sandwiches | Time: 5 minutes

butter
8 slices sourdough bread
4 Tbsp. pesto, divided
8 slices fresh mozzarella
1–2 tomatoes, sliced
spinach leaves, to taste
Balsamic Vinegar Reduction (page 79)

1. Heat a sandwich grill, panini press, or skillet. Butter one slice of bread lightly, and place butter side down on the grill. Top with 1 tablespoon of pesto, 1 slice of cheese, sliced tomatoes, spinach, and another slice of cheese. Drizzle balsamic vinegar carefully over another piece of bread, place on the rest of the sandwich, and butter the other side.

2. Cook until golden brown on both sides. Repeat with remaining sandwiches, and serve warm with tomato soup (page 97).

TURKEY PESTO CRÊPES

Crêpes are to France what hot dog stands are to New York City. They sell them everywhere and not just for breakfast or a tasty dessert. They also make great lunches and dinners! Here is a fun and light French lunch!—Chelsea

Makes 8–10 5-inch sandwiches (serves about 4)
Time: 30 minutes

Crêpes
1 cup flour
2 cups milk
2 eggs
1 Tbsp. brown sugar
2 Tbsp. melted butter
½ tsp. vanilla extract

Turkey Filling
½ cup sun-dried tomatoes
1 lb. sliced turkey
¼ cup diced red onion
½ cup diced red bell pepper
¼ cup diced mushrooms
1 Tbsp. oil
pesto to spread
2 cups shredded cheese (mozzarella or cheddar mix)

1. Mix all crêpe ingredients together until batter is smooth. A hand mixer would be great for this.
2. Spray or butter a medium-sized pan on medium heat. Pour ¼ cup batter on the pan. Tilt pan to spread batter around, leaving a thin layer.
3. Cook for 1–2 minutes and flip.

4. Pile cooked crêpes on a plate.

5. Sauté sun-dried tomatoes, turkey, red onion, red bell pepper, and mushrooms in a separate pan with oil.

6. Spread pesto on a crêpe, sprinkle with cheese, and add ¼ cup of turkey filling to one side. Fold crêpe in half and put back in the crêpe pan (butter pan if needed) on medium heat. Cook both sides until cheese is melted (2 minutes on each side).

If you have extra turkey filling, put it in your eggs in the morning.

Alterations: You can use flour tortillas or bread instead of crêpes.

(use gluten-free flour, but crêpes will be thicker)

(use almond/coconut milk, coconut oil in place of butter, and no cheese)

GRILLED CHEESE ROLLS

This is a great way to make grilled cheese if you're running out of bread, or if you just want to shake it up a bit. Serve with warm tomato soup (page 97).—Ashley

Makes 4 rolls | Time: 5 minutes

4 slices sandwich bread
butter, softened
cheddar cheese,
    grated or sliced

COOKING TIP:
However you like your grilled cheese, try it with this! Add thin slices of tomatoes, peppers, different types of cheese, or anything you like.

1. Heat up a panini press or griddle. Lay bread on a cutting board or other smooth surface. Using a rolling pin, roll bread very flat, as thin as it can go.

2. Lay cheese in a straight line through the middle of the bread. Fold the edges of the bread in, overlapping them, and brush quickly with butter on fold side. Place fold side down on the grill, and brush butter on the other side.

3. Cook until golden brown on both sides and the cheese has melted. Watch carefully as the cheese may ooze out and make a mess if cooked too long.

EASY

GNOCCHI IN HOMEMADE CHEESE SAUCE

This tastes like mac and cheese—only better! The dumplings have an excellent texture in any sauce.

It's good to learn how to make your own sauces so that you know what really goes into them. However, if you need a fast lunch, save some sauce, whether homemade or from the store, and serve over the gnocchi.—Ashley

Makes 2–3 servings | Time: 15 minutes

1 (16-oz.) package potato gnocchi dumplings
3 Tbsp. cornstarch
1 cup chicken broth
2 Tbsp. butter
1½ tsp. minced garlic
1 cup milk
2½ cups grated cheddar cheese
½ cup grated parmesan cheese
salt and pepper, to taste

1. Bring a pot of water to boil and add gnocchi. Cook for about 4 minutes until the dumplings float to the surface. Drain and remove from heat.

2. Whisk the cornstarch and chicken stock together in a bowl until the cornstarch has dissolved. Set aside.

3. In a saucepan or pot, melt butter and add garlic. Sautee for about 2 minutes. Stir in the cornstarch mixture. Add in milk, stirring constantly, and bring mixture to a boil over medium-high heat.

4. Remove from heat and stir in cheeses, whisking constantly until melted and well combined. Season with salt and pepper.

5. Add gnocchi to sauce and stir well. Serve with optional panko or breadcrumbs sprinkled on top.

(without breadcrumbs)

MONTE CRISTO SANDWICHES

If you love French toast, you will love this sandwich stuffed with turkey and veggies, sprinkled with powdered sugar. If you make extra French toast, enjoy it for a breakfast treat!—Chelsea

Makes 4–5 sandwiches | Time: 30 minutes

French Toast

5 eggs
2 tsp. cinnamon
¼ cup milk
1 tsp. vanilla
butter or oil
8–10 slices bread
1½ cups shredded cheese
powdered sugar to sprinkle on top of sandwich

HEALTH TIP:
Coconut oil is much better for you than butter.

Turkey Mix

½ zucchini, sliced
½ green or yellow bell pepper, sliced
½ onion, sliced
2 mushrooms, diced
½ lb. turkey slices or enough for 4–5 sandwiches
1 Tbsp. coconut oil or butter

1. Crack eggs in a sandwich-sized container or a pie pan. Add cinnamon, milk, and vanilla and whisk together.

2. On medium heat, coat a pan with butter or coconut oil. Dip both sides of bread in egg mixture and place in pan. Cook each side for around 4 minutes or until lightly browned.

3. Sauté zucchini, pepper, onion, mushrooms, and turkey with coconut oil or butter for 5 minutes in a separate pan on medium heat.

4. Place turkey mix and cheese between French toast slices. Place the sandwich back in the pan. Allow cheese to melt on medium heat for 1½ minutes on each side.

5. Butter top of sandwich then sprinkle with powdered sugar.

(minus butter, cheese, and milk—use almond milk to replace milk)   (with gluten-free bread)

ITALIAN TURKEY GRILLED CHEESE SANDWICHES

Here is a new recipe to add to your quick grilled cheese arsenal.—Chelsea

Makes 4 sandwiches | Time: 15–20 Minutes

pesto to spread
8 bread slices
2 cups shredded cheese (mozzarella preferred)
½ lb. sliced turkey
1 Tbsp. butter

1. Spread pesto on one side of each slice of bread.
2. Add a layer of cheese, turkey slices, and then another layer of cheese.
3. Butter a pan and grill sandwich on high for 2 minutes on each side, or until cheese is melted.

Alteration: You can sauté veggies, like red bell peppers, mushrooms, zucchini, and tomatoes in oil and include them in the sandwich.

(without cheese)   (with gluten-free bread)

PIADINAS

These are based off of an Italian street food wrap, which makes them nice for on-the-go eating. If you're in a hurry, shred leftover chicken and use leftover spaghetti noodles in place of the angel hair pasta. Don't worry if they're already covered in sauce; the aioli goes well with marinara!

The wraps I use are as Italian-flavored as I can get from my local store and oval-shaped, but plain flour tortillas will work. I have also baked uncooked tortillas in a skillet with a little olive oil to help the flavors blend better.—Ashley

Makes 4 wraps | Time: 15 minutes

½ recipe Rosemary Lemon Chicken, shredded (page 101)
    OR 1½ cup shredded rotisserie chicken
angel hair pasta, cooked
2 roma tomatoes, diced
½ Tbsp. olive oil
greens and veggies of your choice:
olives
spinach
fresh basil leaves
red onion
sun-dried tomatoes

HEALTH TIP:
Feta cheese has to be at least 70% sheep's milk. If this is sufficient for non-cow dairy needs, use this. If not, use goat's cheese.

aioli or sauce of choice
crumbled feta or goat cheese, to taste
4 flat tortilla wraps, as plain-flavored or Italian-flavored as possible

Lemon Garlic Aioli

2 Tbsp. mayonnaise
2 tsp. pesto
2 tsp. minced garlic cloves
1 tsp. lemon juice

1 pinch salt
½ tsp. pepper

1. In a bowl, mix all aioli ingredients with a spoon until well-blended and set aside.

2. In a separate small bowl, mix roma tomatoes with olive oil. Set aside.

3. Lay out the ingredients in an assembly line in the following order: wraps, pasta, meat, vegetables, sauce, cheese. Create wrap with desired ingredients. When the wrap has been fully loaded, fold in the top and bottom over the filling. Take the left side and fold it over the filling, tucking the edge in under the pasta. Roll to the right, forming a neat burrito.

4. Slice in half and enjoy!

If you aren't making 4 piadinas at once, cover and refrigerate the other ingredients for a few days.

BUFFALO CHICKEN TACOS

This spicy recipe will be one of your favorites if you are a buffalo sauce fan!—Chelsea

Makes 10 tacos | Time: 30 Minutes

*3 boneless, skinless chicken breasts
2 Tbsp. oil, divided
1 (15.25-oz.) can corn
⅔ cup buffalo sauce
1 avocado, sliced
10 corn tortillas
3 cups sliced Romaine lettuce
ranch dressing to drizzle
1 cup shredded cheese

1.   Heat 1 tablespoon of oil in a pan on medium-high heat. Add chicken and cook for 7–8 minutes. Drain excess water. Shred or dice chicken and set aside.

2.   Drain corn and add to a pan with 1 tablespoon of oil. Cook until corn starts to brown. Mix in buffalo sauce and chicken.

3.   Warm up tortillas in a damp cloth in the microwave.

4.   Add desired ingredients to corn tortilla. Drizzle ranch and sprinkle cheese on top.

2–3 cans of chicken will also work.

Alterations: To make it less spicy, add less buffalo sauce and more ranch. You can also use flour tortillas instead of corn.

(no cheese or
ranch dressing)

SPICY TURKEY QUESADILLAS

This is a fun, tasty, and quick recipe when you only have a small window of time to make good food.—Chelsea

Makes 4 quesadillas | Time: 10–15 minutes
(depends on how many you want to make)

8 flour tortillas
2 cups shredded cheese
½–1 cup spicy salsa
1 lb. turkey, sliced
3 oz. (2 cups) spinach
butter or cooking spray

1. Butter a pan on medium heat. Place tortilla (or as many will fit in your pan) with a layer of cheese, speckled with salsa, several slices of turkey, small handful of spinach, more cheese, and then another tortilla on top.
2. Cook both sides until lightly brown and cheese is all melted.

(with gluten-free
or corn tortillas)

CHICKEN SOUVLAKI

Though truly authentic is always the best, homemade Greek food is delicious and money-saving! After soaking in a marinade, this tasty and tangy chicken practically falls off the skewer! You can also pop the meat into a gyro (page 50), a piadina (page 44), or a soup.—Ashley

Makes 2 skewers | Time: 40 minutes

3 Tbsp. lemon juice
3 sprigs of fresh thyme or about ½ tsp. dried
4 cloves garlic
½ tsp. oregano
½ tsp. salt
2 tsp. olive oil
1 boneless, skinless chicken breast, sliced or cubed
bamboo skewers, soaked
soaking the skewers for at least 10 minutes beforehand keeps them from scorching in the oven or while you're grilling
grape tomatoes

1. Stir together lemon juice, thyme, garlic, oregano, salt, and olive oil in a sealed plastic bag. Add chicken and shake to coat well. Refrigerate for at least 30 minutes. If you have the time, allow to marinate for a few hours.

2. Thread chicken onto skewers, weaving back and forth if sliced. Thread a few grape tomatoes onto the skewer as well.

3. Grill over medium-high heat until cooked through. Brush any leftover marinade over the chicken during the last 5 minutes of cooking. Serve with pilafi rice (page 187).

If you do not have access to a grill, place the skewers

on a baking sheet and preheat the oven to 325 degrees. Bake the skewers until done through, which should be about 20 minutes. Check for doneness, and don't over-cook. The chicken should be at least 160 degrees if you have a meat thermometer, or it should feel firm if you do not.

TIME-SAVING TIP:
If you come home in the middle of the day, put the chicken in the marinade before you leave in the morning. Then grill once you get home and have a quick, easy lunch!

CHICKEN GYRO

Eat on-the-go like you just visited a great Greek restaurant, without the price! The fries in this sandwich lend great starch and texture to it. If you need to cut out the fat and starch, you can leave them out. But if you can, I recommend you give them a shot!—Ashley

Makes 6 gyros | Time: 5 minutes

6–8 slices of thin pita bread (not pocket pita)
cabbage mixture, finely shredded
1 recipe Chicken Souvlaki (page 48)
2 tomatoes, sliced
1 medium red onion, sliced or diced according to preference
banana peppers, sliced, optional
thin French fries, cooked
½ cup tzatziki sauce

1. Spread cabbage mixture on each pita, to taste. Top with chicken, distributing mostly through the center. Top with tomatoes, veggies, and French fries. Drizzle tzatziki sauce over each pita. Take both sides of 1 pita and roll in over the fillings, pressing in to keep the gyro together. Wrap up in aluminum foil, placed diagonally under the gyro, and serve.

(without tzatziki sauce)   (without the fries)

TZATZIKI SAUCE

Cool and creamy tzatziki perfectly complements souvlaki or gyro as a spread. Or, pile it in a bowl and serve as a dip!—Ashley

3 Tbsp. olive oil
1 Tbsp. vinegar
2 cloves garlic, minced
½ tsp. salt
¼ tsp. pepper
1 cup Greek yogurt, strained
1 cup sour cream
2 cucumbers, peeled, seeded, and diced

1. Combine oil, vinegar, garlic, salt, and pepper in a bowl. Mix until combined.

2. Whisk the yogurt and sour cream together. Add the olive oil mixture and whisk well.

3. Add cucumber, and pour the whole mixture into a food processor, pulsing until smooth. Chill for 2 hours before serving.

SWEDISH MEATBALLS IN CREAM SAUCE

The easiest way to make these is to use pre-made meatballs from the freezer aisle. I'm addicted to the cream sauce! I never realized that the secret to making it myself was soy sauce. You can add more or less to taste.—Ashley

Makes 5–6 servings | Time: 25 minutes

1 (16-oz.) bag Swedish meatballs
1 Tbsp. butter
1 Tbsp. flour
1 cup beef broth
½ cup half-and-half
2 Tbsp. milk
¼ tsp. soy sauce
thyme, to taste
½ tsp. allspice
½ tsp. onion powder
salt and pepper, to taste

1. Preheat oven according to meatball package. Prepare a baking sheet with 1-inch edges, and lay meatballs in a single layer across baking sheet. Bake according to directions.

2. In a saucepan, melt butter over medium heat and add flour. Whisk until golden brown and flour is cooked.

3. Add beef stock and half-and-half. Whisk in soy sauce and spices, and simmer until thickened. Pour over meatballs, and serve with pasta if desired.

AVOCADO TUNA SANDWICH

Avocado is a much healthier addition to your tuna sandwich than mayonnaise. And tasty!—Chelsea

Makes 2 sandwiches | Time: 5–8 minutes

1 (5-oz.) can tuna, drained
1 ripe avocado (a bit more if you want to use it as a spread as well)
4 bread slices
2 slices cheddar cheese

Optional Toppings:
lettuce
tomato
mayonnaise or ranch

> **HEALTH TIP:**
> Avocados are full of fiber and have more potassium than bananas..

1. In a small bowl mash a pitted and peeled avocado with a fork, then mix in tuna.

2. Spread a bit of extra avocado on each slice of bread. Then add sliced cheese and ½ tuna spread on each sandwich.

3. Add optional sliced tomato or lettuce to sandwich. (Use mayonnaise or ranch on each slice if you want bread to be more moist.)

(without cheese)   (with gluten-free bread)   (without mayonnaise)

CRAZY-GOOD TUNA MELT

When tuna comes cheap, tuna sandwiches become a staple. However, there are ways to make a typical sandwich more appealing and keep you from growing bored! A dash of lemon juice, I've found, does the trick nicely.—Ashley

Makes 2 sandwiches | Time: 5 minutes

1 (5-oz.) can tuna
2 Tbsp. mayonnaise
½ tsp. lemon juice
salt and pepper, to taste
4 slices bread
butter
4 slices cheddar cheese

1.   Heat a panini press or griddle. In a bowl, mix tuna, mayonnaise, lemon juice, cilantro, and salt and pepper until well combined.

2.   Butter one side of each bread slice and lay on the griddle. Spread tuna on bread and top with a slice of cheddar cheese. Top with another buttered slice of bread.

3.   Grill on both sides until cheese has melted and serve warm.

Variations: Add a dash of sriracha instead of lemon for a spicy tuna salad.

Add 2 Tbsp. chopped cilantro and replace the lemon juice with lime. Alternately, add Dijon mustard instead of juice.

Try relish, chopped celery, or herbs for a fresh and healthy version!

(with goat or feta cheese)

ONIGIRI (SPICY TUNA ROLL)

This Japanese food is a great way to use up leftover rice and tastes a bit like sushi when done. The trick is that it has to be very sticky or glutinous, or it will fall apart. The best is sushi rice, but I've made it work with leftover jasmine rice. A more authentic onigiri has a rectangle of nori (seaweed) around the base. It's a fun addition if you do have it or know someone who keeps it around, but it also is not strictly necessary.—Ashley

Makes 4–5 rolls | Time: 10 minutes

1 (5-oz.) can tuna
2 Tbsp. mayonnaise
sriracha, to taste
1 scallion, chopped
1 avocado, sliced
4 cups leftover white sticky rice, divided
Nori, sliced into rectangles, optional
sesame seeds, optional
soy sauce, for serving

1. In a small bowl, mix the tuna, mayonnaise, and sriracha. Stir in the chopped scallions.

2. Gather ½ cup rice in the palm of your hand and form a patty. Place about 1½ tablespoons of tuna mixture in a ball into the patty, and add avocado slices to taste. Take another ⅓ cup rice and top over the patty, sealing the edges. Cupping your hands, form the patty into a triangle shape. If you have any, wrap the bottom side with a rectangle of nori.

3. Repeat with the remaining rice until you have 4–5 patties. Sprinkle with sesame seeds if you have them, and serve with a dipper of soy sauce.

COCONUT CHICKEN STRIPS

Adding sweet coconut and baking these chicken strips turns a classic into a healthy, quick meal. Serve with a strong, spicy dipping sauce to add a burst of flavor that makes these incredibly addicting.—Ashley

Makes about 15 strips | Time: 30 minutes

3 boneless, skinless chicken breasts
½ cup flour
salt and pepper, to taste
1 pinch curry powder
1 egg with 1 Tbsp. water
sweetened coconut flakes
sweet chili sauce or Mango Cilantro Dipping Sauce (recipe
    below)

1. Preheat oven to 400 degrees.

2. Slice chicken breasts into thin strips (about 5 per breast). Combine flour, salt, pepper, and curry powder in a bowl. One at a time, dredge each chicken strip in the mixture. Then dip in egg mixture, and allow excess to drip off. Finally, coat chicken in coconut flakes and lay on a baking sheet.

3. Bake chicken for 15–20 minutes or until chicken is done. Serve with chili sauce or mango sauce.

4. If you have access to a heavy skillet or deep fryer, these can be fried rather than baked. Fry in batches of 4–5 for about 2 minutes until deep golden brown. Remove with tongs and place on a plate covered with a paper towel.

(with rice flour)

Mango Cilantro Dipping Sauce

Sweet and just a touch spicy, this sauce goes great with chicken. If desired, add a little more mango and sriracha to boost the flavor.—Ashley

Makes about 1 cup | Time: 5 minutes

½ cup mayonnaise
1 mango, cut into chunks
2 Tbsp. fresh cilantro
1 Tbsp. honey
1 pinch curry powder
sriracha, to taste (a couple of drops should do it)
½ tsp. lemon juice

1. Mix all ingredients in a food processor, and blend until cilantro is completely mixed in. Store in an airtight container for up to a couple of days.

RAMEN STIR FRY

Some days, even with your best efforts, ramen noodles are all you have. Maybe they're left over from the days before you bought this cookbook! Here's a good way to use them up and get a better meal than making them the old-fashioned way.—Ashley

Makes 1–2 servings | Time: 15 minutes

½ Tbsp. olive oil
1 clove garlic, minced
1 boneless, skinless chicken breast, cubed
1 tsp. soy sauce
1 tsp. Worcestershire sauce
⅓ cup frozen veggie mix OR red bell peppers, julienned
1 block ramen noodles, beef or pork flavor
1 egg
salt and pepper

1. Heat olive oil in a skillet or wok over medium heat. Add garlic and sauté until fragrant. Stir in chicken, soy sauce, Worcestershire, and veggies. Cook until chicken is done through and juices run clear.

2. Meanwhile, in a separate bowl or saucepan, boil ramen noodles until just done. Drain and remove from heat.

3. Once the vegetables are almost done in the other pan, crack in the egg. Stir to scramble.

4. Add ramen noodles and seasoning packet that came with it to stir fry pan. Stir well. If necessary to get the flavor onto all the noodles, add about 1 tablespoon water. Serve.

CHICKEN SPRING ROLLS AND PEANUT SAUCE

Enjoy this light and tasty classic Asian dish! This lunch will help you walk away satisfied, still licking the peanut sauce off your fingers.—Chelsea

Makes 10 spring rolls | Time: 30–40 minutes

2 boneless, skinless chicken breasts, thinly sliced
1 Tbsp. oil (coconut or avocado oil is the best!)
2 cups cooked rice
1 yellow or red bell pepper, thinly sliced
1 cup thinly sliced carrots
½ cucumber, peeled and thinly sliced (hotdog style)
3 romaine lettuce leaves, thinly sliced
1 cup thinly sliced purple cabbage
10 rice paper rounds (located in the Asian section of a grocery store)

Peanut Sauce
⅓ cup creamy peanut butter
2½ Tbsp. brown sugar
1 Tbsp. lime juice
1 Tbsp. soy sauce
1 tsp. peeled and finely minced ginger
1 tsp. sriracha
2 Tbsp. hot water

1. Cook chicken in oil on medium-high heat for 7–10 minutes.
2. With all veggies, chicken, and rice prepared, follow the package directions to soak rice paper.
3. Place soaked rice paper on a plate and put desired

ingredients in the middle of 1 round. Fold in opposite edges and then roll everything up tightly.

4. Put finished spring rolls on a plate, seam side down.

5. Mix all ingredients for the peanut dipping sauce and then enjoy!

(with gluten-free
soy sauce)

BBQ RICE

Want a fun new take on a rice bowl? Try this veggie packed and BBQ flavored rice recipe.—Chelsea

Makes 4 servings | Time: 20–30 minutes

2 boneless, skinless chicken breasts, diced
2 Tbsp. oil, divided
2 cups frozen mixed veggies
4 cups cooked rice
½–¾ cup BBQ Sauce

HEALTH TIP:
Avoid BBQ sauce with high fructose corn syrup.

1. Heat 1 tablespoon oil on medium-high heat. Then add chicken and cook for 7 minutes. Drain excess water.

2. Run veggies under hot water to help them thaw. Then add veggies to chicken pan with 1 more tablespoon oil. Cook for about 5 more minutes. Mix in rice and BBQ sauce.

HAWAIIAN CHICKEN WRAPS

This summer wrap is sweet and healthy! Perfect to last several days as a quick and delicious lunch. You can also have it with toast instead of a tortilla or in a lettuce wrap.—Chelsea

Makes 4–5 wraps | Time: 15–20 minutes

1 Tbsp. oil (recommend coconut oil)
½ cup diced pineapple chunks
1 (12.5-oz.) can chicken breast chunks
½ red bell pepper, sliced
½ cup sliced zucchini
½ cup diced sweet onion
4–5 flour tortillas
1 cup cheese

Optional Toppings:
lettuce
tomato slices
BBQ sauce

1. In a medium size pan, add oil and pineapple on medium-high heat. After about 3 minutes add chicken chunks. Stir occasionally. Cook until pineapple is slightly blackened. Then add red bell pepper, zucchini, and sweet onion. Sauté for 3–4 minutes.

2. Cover 1 tortilla in cheese and melt in the micro-wave or in a pan. Add desired amount of the Hawaiian mixture then include desired toppings with a drizzle of BBQ sauce. Roll up tortilla and enjoy!

(without cheese)   (use gluten-free
                                     bread or corn tortillas
                                     or lettuce wrap)

HAWAIIAN MACARONI SALAD

A creamy, addicting favorite of Hawaiian restaurants, this recipe will make you dream of Pacific islands! It is essential to use real mayonnaise for the best, richest flavor.—Ashley

Makes 3–5 servings | Time: 10 minutes

3 cups macaroni
¼ cup grated carrot
1 cup mayonnaise
¼ cup milk
2 Tbsp. sweetened condensed milk
salt and pepper, to taste

1. Bring water to a boil in a pot, and cook macaroni until noodles are tender. Drain and set aside to cool completely.

2. Combine carrot, mayonnaise, milk, and salt and pepper in a bowl. Mix in macaroni until well-coated. Chill in refrigerator before serving.

Inbetweeners and Snacks

WHITE CHEDDAR POPCORN

This popcorn can either be enjoyed plain, or with the cheddar powder. I found mine from a local Amish market, but it is available in other large supermarkets. It'll last—but only as long as you can resist making this delicious popcorn!—Ashley

Makes 8 cups popped corn | Time: 5 minutes

1 Tbsp. coconut oil
¼ cup popcorn kernels
white cheddar powder, to taste

1. In a pot with a lid, heat the coconut oil over medium-high heat. Add three popcorn kernels. The oil is ready when these three have popped.
2. Add the popcorn kernels and cover with a lid. Shake every so often to pop as many as possible. When the space between pops reaches about 3 seconds, remove from heat and pour into a bowl.
3. Sprinkle with white cheddar powder, tossing to coat between shakes of powder, and enjoy.

(without the
  powder)

MACARONI BOMBS

Use these either as a meal (like macaroni casserole made finger food), or as a cheesy, gooey side. Serve with sauce if you would like an extra kick of flavor.—Ashley

Makes 15–20 | Time: 25 minutes

1 pkg. cooked macaroni with cheese sauce
¼ cup shredded parmesan
¼ cup shredded mozzarella
1 egg
1 tsp. water
1½ cups panko or bread crumbs
marinara sauce

> **COOKING TIP:**
> If your pasta doesn't stick together well enough to form a ball, heat in the microwave for 30 second to 1 minute. It should then be sticky enough to hold its shape.

1. Preheat oven to 400 degrees. Make sure the macaroni you are using is completely cool by the time you start, or it will not hold its shape.
2. Take small handfuls of pasta and roll into balls.
3. In a small dish, mix egg and water. Dip each macaroni ball into the egg, and let the excess drip off. Roll in the panko or bread crumbs until fully coated.
4. Place the coated macaroni bombs on a baking sheet, and bake for about 15 minutes. Serve warm with marinara sauce.

Variation: These can also be fried. Heat oil to 375 degrees and fry 4–5 at a time until golden brown.

DELICIOUSLY WHIPPED APPLE DIP

McKell Parsons introduced me to this perfect dip for a party or when you just really have a sweet tooth!—Chelsea

Makes 1 small bowl | Time: 5 minutes

1 (8-oz.) package whipped cream cheese
3½ Tbsp. brown sugar
2½ Tbsp. Heath toffee bits
about 4 apples

COOKING TIP:
Apples brown easily. Only eat what you need or add a couple squirts of lime or lemon juice to prevent browning.

1. Mix all ingredients apart from apples together in a bowl.
2. Cut apples in small slices. Dip and eat!

CHOCOLATE CHIP PEANUT BUTTER ENERGY BITES

If you want a quick power snack, eat one of these—or a few!—Chelsea

Makes 18 bites | Time: 5 minutes prep, 15 minutes freeze

1 cup rolled oats
½ cup chunky peanut butter
½ cup mini semi-sweet chocolate chips
⅓ cup raw honey
¼ cup ground flaxseed
½ tsp. vanilla

HEALTH TIP:
Flaxseeds are full of Omega-3 fatty acids, which play a large part in heart health. You can find flaxseed in the baking section of your grocery store.

1. Mix all ingredients in a small bowl.
2. Roll up spoon-sized balls and place on a cookie sheet. Put cookie sheet in freezer for 15 minutes.
3. Pull out and enjoy! Keep leftovers in freezer.

(gluten-free rolled oats)   (without chocolate chips)

GUACAMOLE

Grab some chips and guacamole and enjoy your snack! This recipe is also a fantastic topping to many of the Hispanic dishes in this book.—Chelsea

Makes about 2½ cups | Time: 10 minutes

3 ripe avocados
½ cup diced red onion
½ cup diced tomato
½ tsp. garlic powder
½ tsp. salt
½ Tbsp. lime juice

1. Cut avocados in half, pull out pits, scoop out avocado pulp, and place into a bowl. Mash with a fork. Add all other ingredients and mix together.
2. Eat with tortilla chips!

STINKIN' EASY 7-LAYER DIP

Need to contribute something to a party, but only have a couple minutes to throw something edible together? Have no fear! The 7-Layer Dip is here!—Chelsea

1 (16-oz.) can refried beans
2 cup guacamole (store-bought) OR the guacamole recipe
    from page 70
1 cup sour cream
1 cup salsa
¼ cup sliced olives
1 green onion, thinly sliced
1 cup shredded cheese

1. Spread the beans out evenly in an 8 x 8 pan. Add an even layer of guacamole, sour cream, and salsa. Sprinkle a layer of cheese, olives, and green onions.

BRUSCHETTA

Savory, crunchy, and creamy all at once, these are excellent for lunch or for party sides.—Ashley

Makes 10–15 pieces | Time: 5 minutes

1 (8-oz.) pkg. cream cheese
½ cup mayonnaise
1 pkg. ranch dressing mix
½ tsp. dill
2–3 Roma tomatoes, diced
olive oil
½ Tbsp. dry basil
1 crusty baguette

1. In a bowl, combine cream cheese, mayonnaise, ranch mix, and dill until smooth. In another bowl, combine tomatoes, oil, and basil.

2. Slice baguette about 1 inch thick and spread with ranch mixture. Top with tomato mixture and serve.

SOUPS AND SALADS

PIZZA SALAD

If you are craving pizza but have already had it four times this week, this salad is a healthy and satisfying alternative. The creamy marinara dressing with nearly all the pizza ingredients will make this a favorite. Zucchini Breadsticks (page 194) are also a wonderful addition to this meal.—Chelsea

Makes 2–3 servings | Time: 10–15 minutes

Salad:
1 head romaine lettuce, chopped
½ cup sliced olives
½ cup diced green or yellow bell pepper
½ cup diced red onion
½ cup diced tomato
½ cup mozzarella cheese
as many slices pepperoni as you want

Dressing:
2 Tbsp. ranch
4 Tbsp. marinara sauce

HEALTH TIP:
Use chicken as a healthier alternative to pepperoni.

1. Mix all salad ingredients in a medium bowl.
2. Add ranch and marinara sauce to a small bowl and mix. Add the amount of desired dressing to your individual salad.

SWEET GARDEN SALAD

Add mandarin oranges and apple bits to your freshly tossed salad for an extra sweet taste amidst all those veggies. I recommend adding Paprika Brown Sugar Chicken (page 100) with honey mustard dressing to this salad.—Chelsea

Makes 2–3 servings | Time: 10–15 minutes

1 large head romaine lettuce, sliced
½ cup mandarin oranges (from a can)
½ cup diced apple
½ cup diced green or yellow bell pepper
½ cup chopped carrots
½ cup diced sweet onion
½ cup diced tomato
sprinkle with shredded cheese
a handful of smashed nuts (almonds or cashews), optional

1. Mix all salad ingredients except shredded cheese in a medium bowl.
2. Add shredded cheese to individual plate and drizzle your favorite dressing on top.

(depending on dressing
and without cheese)

TACO SALAD

This is a filling salad for you and your roommates to enjoy!—Chelsea

Makes 4 servings | Time: 20 minutes

1 lb. lean ground beef
1 taco seasoning packet
1½–2 heads romaine lettuce, chopped
¼ cup diced black olives
½ cup diced red onion
½ cup chopped carrots
½ cup diced green or orange bell pepper
½ cup diced tomatoes
½ cup drained corn, (I normally get frozen corn and then thaw it under hot water)
¾ cup rinsed and drained black beans

Toppings:
shredded cheese
ranch dressing
salsa
avocado or guacamole (page 70)

1. Brown ground beef in a pan and soak up fat with paper towels. Follow instructions on taco seasoning packet.
2. Mix lettuce, black olives, red onion, carrots, bell pepper, tomato, corn, and black beans in a medium-sized bowl.
3. Add desired amount to plate and add beef (I recommend about ⅓ cup), cheese, ranch dressing, salsa, and avocado (or guacamole). Stir together and eat!

(exclude
cheese and
ranch)

(check taco
seasoning
packet)

BUFFALO RANCH CHICKEN SALAD

Try this quick and flavorful salad with just the right amount of creaminess and spice.—Chelsea

Makes 2 servings | Time: 15 minutes

1½ heads romaine lettuce, chopped
1 (12-oz.) can chicken, drained
¼ cup Frank's RedHot Buffalo Wing Sauce
½ cup drained corn
½ cup rinsed and drained black beans
¼ cup chopped sweet onion
½ chopped red bell pepper
½ pitted, peeled, and diced avocado
½ cup shredded cheddar cheese
ranch dressing

1. Mix chicken and sauce in a small bowl.
2. Place chicken and all other ingredients in a medium bowl and gently mix.
3. Add ranch dressing to your individual salad.

CAPRESE

Make a quick Italian salad from tomatoes, cheese, and basil. It tastes as good as it looks!—Ashley

Makes 1–2 servings | Time: 5 minutes

2–3 roma tomatoes
8 oz. fresh mozzarella, sliced thickly
½ cup fresh basil leaves
olive oil
⅓ cup balsamic vinegar reduction.
salt and pepper, optional

1. Slice tomatoes about ½ inch thick. Toss in a salad or serving bowl with cheese and basil.
2. Drizzle with olive oil and balsamic reduction. Sprinkle with salt and pepper, and serve fresh.

(if using goat cheese)

BALSAMIC VINEGAR REDUCTION

By sweetening and thickening good balsamic vinegar, you can create an excellent salad dressing, marinade, or—interestingly enough—ice cream topping!

Use thinner reductions for drizzling over salads or as marinades, and thicker reductions for ice cream or caprese (page 78).—Ashley

Makes ⅓ to ¾ cup | Time: 15 minutes

1 cup balsamic vinegar
¼ cup honey

1. Combine balsamic vinegar and honey in a saucepan and bring to a high simmer. Simmer until the mixture has reduced and it coats a spoon. You can continue to cook until desired thickness, but do not reduce to less than ⅓ cup or it will burn. Set aside to cool. It will thicken considerably once cooled.

Variations: There are a number of spices and flavoring agents you can add! Try cinnamon and cloves for a sweet reduction.

ROASTED VEGGIE AND CHICKEN CHOWDER

Enjoy this warm, creamy pot of heaven. Perfect for those chilly nights when all you want is a blanket and an awesome movie.—Chelsea

Makes 6-7 servings | Time: 30–45 minutes

2 cups almond milk
1 (13-oz.) can evaporated milk
¼ cup milk
4 cups water
8 tsp. chicken bouillon (recommend Better-Than-Bouillon brand)
5 small potatoes, diced
1–2 tsp. black pepper
½ tsp. salt
2 Tbsp. oil, divided
2 boneless, skinless chicken breasts, diced
2 cups frozen veggie mix (carrots, corn, etc.), thawed
1 red bell pepper, chopped
4 green onions, thinly sliced rounds
2 tsp. dried parsley

1. Add almond milk, evaporated milk, water, bouillon, diced potatoes, black pepper, and salt in a large pot on medium-high heat. Cover pot and heat on medium.

2. In a medium-sized pan, add 1 tablespoon of oil and diced chicken on medium-high heat. Cook chicken for 6–7 minutes. Drain excess liquid then add to pot.

3. In the same medium-sized pan, heat 1 tablespoon of oil and add thawed mixed veggies and red bell pepper. Sauté until slightly blackened, about 8 minutes. Add veggies to pot.

4. Add green onions and parsley to the pot and mix. Check to make sure potatoes are soft and then serve!

SPICY CHICKEN SOUP

This takes chicken soup to a new taste level! This is cheap, easy, and absolutely delicious. Recommend melting cheese in a tortilla and dipping it in the soup! Unless you love really spicy soup, the Mexican table cream or "crema" is a must have.—Chelsea

Makes 5–6 servings | Time: 35–40 minutes

2 large chicken breasts, sliced
1 Tbsp. oil
8 cups water
3 Tbsp. chicken bullion (recommend Better-Than-Bouillon brand)
1 tsp. paprika
1 tsp. black pepper
1 tsp. cumin
2 Tbsp. dried parsley
1 (15-oz.) can black beans, drained and rinsed
1 (15.25-oz.)can corn, undrained
1 (10-oz.) can Rotel tomatoes with chilis (for less spicy use 1 can Mexican stewed tomatoes)
½ cup diced onion
½ green bell pepper, diced
crema (Mexican table cream) or sour cream

1. Cook sliced chicken in oil for 7–8 minutes. Once chicken is cooked, shred.

2. Add remaining ingredients into a pot. Turn on high and stir occasionally. Once soup begins to boil, turn on medium for 3 more minutes and add the shredded chicken.

3. (I recommend adding 2 tablespoons of crema or sour cream to each serving bowl.)

Variation: Add 2 cups cooked wild rice to soup.

(though limit
your crema)

TACO SOUP

This is one of those soups you can throw in a Crock-Pot in minutes and walk away. It is a perfect meal to help you survive your finals week. It seems like a lot of salsa, but this recipe makes a large amount of food that is awesome to freeze and eat later.—Chelsea

Makes 5–6 servings | Time: 3 hours

2 large chicken breasts, frozen
1 (14.5-oz.) can Mexican stewed tomatoes, squished
1 (15.25-oz.) can corn, undrained
1 (15-oz.) can black beans, rinsed and drained
1 (15.25-oz.) can kidney beans, rinsed and drained
1 (6-oz.) can black olives, sliced
1 (64-oz.) jar salsa (I use Pace mild or medium.)

Toppings:
1 avocado, pitted, peeled, and diced
crema or sour cream
shredded cheese
tortilla chips

> **TIME-SAVING TIP:**
> You can also cook chicken in a pan, add everything to a pot, and heat it up. It will only take you about half an hour. Stir soup frequently so it doesn't burn.

1. Dump frozen chicken, squished Mexican stewed tomatoes, corn, black beans, kidney beans, sliced olives, and salsa in a Crock-Pot. Turn Crock-Pot on high and leave for three hours.
2. After three hours, pull out chicken and dice. Return chicken to Crock-Pot and mix. Drop temperature to low.
3. Dish out soup and add desired toppings!

(without cheese and sour cream)

CHICKEN AND GNOCCHI SOUP

This recipe was originally inspired by Olive Garden's similar soup, and you can make a lot more of it for your time and money. It has come a long way from its restaurant-based origins, and now my friends and family rave over this recipe—and would rather have this than go out any day!—Ashley

Makes 5–6 servings | Time: 40 minutes

¼ cup unsalted butter
1 medium yellow onion, diced
2 Tbsp. cornstarch OR ¼ cup flour
6 cups chicken broth
6–7 large fresh basil leaves OR 2 tsp. dried basil
1 tsp. minced or crushed garlic
1 cup sliced carrot
2 stalks celery, diced

1 Tbsp. olive oil
2 boneless, skinless chicken breasts, cubed
1 Tbsp. Montreal chicken seasoning
2 tsp. lemon juice
salt and pepper to taste

1 (16-oz.) package gnocchi dumplings
1 pint heavy cream

DAIRY-FREE TIP:
Try coconut milk in place of heavy cream. It will be sweeter, so add another teaspoon of bouillon. You can hardly tell the difference!

1. Melt butter in a medium skillet. Add onion and cook until translucent. Add cornstarch to create a roux, stirring until creamy and lump-free. Transfer to a large pot.

2. Stir in chicken broth over medium-high heat. Add carrots, basil, and garlic. Let simmer for 30 minutes.

3. Meanwhile, in a medium skillet, heat oil and add chicken. Scatter seasoning and lemon juice over meat and cook until juices run clear and chicken is done through. Add chicken to soup and continue simmering until above 30 minutes are done.

4. Add salt and pepper to taste, and raise temperature to a boil. Add gnocchi to soup and cook until the dumplings float to the surface. Remove from heat and add cream, stirring until well combined. Serve immediately with artisan bread.

Alternately, make ahead by transferring to a large slow cooker and allowing to simmer on medium for 3–5 hours. Add gnocchi twenty minutes before and cream five minutes before serving.

(without cream)

TOMATO TORTELLINI SOUP

This hearty soup makes a very large amount, but it stores well for a few days. Split with your roommates if you want help finishing it! For a non-dairy option, this soup is still very excellent without the cream and cheese. Instead, add noodles of your choice and cook those in place of the cheese tortellini.—Ashley

Makes 5–6 servings | Time: 15 minutes

2 (10.75 oz.) cans condensed tomato soup
1 can condensed tomato bisque soup, optional
4 cups chicken broth
½ cup chopped sun-dried tomatoes
1 tsp. onion powder
1 Tbsp. Italian seasoning
½ tsp. salt
½ tsp. pepper
1 (9-oz.) package cheese tortellini
1 pint heavy or whipping cream
½ cup shredded parmesan cheese

> **GLUTEN-FREE TIP:**
> Regular condensed tomato soup is not gluten-free!

> **DAIRY-FREE TIP:**
> Try coconut milk in place of heavy cream. It will be sweeter, so add another teaspoon of bouillon. You can hardly tell the difference!

1. In a large pot or Crock-Pot, combine the soup, broth, tomatoes, and seasonings. Heat to a boil, stirring frequently. Add tortellini to soup. Cook tortellini until done, about 5 minutes.

2. Pour cream into soup, stirring while doing so. Stir in parmesan cheese, and serve warm.

(with gluten-free condensed tomato soup)   (without cream or cheese)

LASAGNA SOUP

This soup has a rich meaty taste mixed with the subtle accents of some well-placed spices. The list of ingredients may look overwhelming, but most of them are small amounts of simple spices. You are making your own sauce! Don't give up!—Chelsea

Makes 5–6 servings | Time: 40 minutes

9 lasagna noodles
½ lb. lean ground beef
walt and pepper for extra flavor
1 cup diced sweet onion
½ cup diced green or yellow bell pepper
1 garlic clove, minced
1 Tbsp. oil (avocado oil recommended)
4 cups water
1½ tsp. beef bouillon (Better Than Bouillon is the best brand!)
1 can Italian stewed tomatoes
½ cup diced tomatoes
4½ Tbsp. tomato paste
2 cups frozen mixed veggies (Or add 1 cup diced mushrooms and 1 cup diced zucchini)
½ tsp. dried rosemary
2 tsp. dried basil
½ tsp. dried thyme
1 tsp. dried oregano
1 tsp. white sugar
1 Tbsp. Italian seasoning
shredded mozzarella or cheddar cheese

    1. Break the lasagna noodles into bite-size pieces in a large pot and follow the directions on the package.
    2. Brown ground beef over medium heat. Drain fat.

Sprinkle with salt and pepper and then place meat in another bowl.

3. Use the same pan and sauté onion, bell pepper, and garlic (and mushrooms and zucchini if you chose that option) for 4 minutes on medium heat in oil.

4. Once noodles are done, drain and rinse with cold water. Use pot (without noodles) and add water, bouillon, stewed tomatoes (squish with hand), diced tomatoes, tomato paste, frozen veggies, rosemary, basil, thyme, oregano, sugar, and Italian seasoning. Simmer until veggies are thawed and hot. Then add noodles and turn stove on low for a couple minutes and stir.

5. Dish up your soup and add a handful of shredded cheese.

(without cheese)　　　　　(with gluten-free noodles)

ORANGE CHICKEN SOUP

The unique curry and orange flavorings mixed with delicious fruits and vegetables will give your immune system a little extra boost to help you recover from or ward off those nasty colds.—Chelsea

Makes 4–5 servings | Time: 45 minutes

1 large boneless, skinless chicken breast
1 Tbsp. oil (avocado oil is fantastic)
5 cups water
2 cups orange juice (high pulp)
2 Tbsp. chicken bouillon (Better Than Bouillon brand is the best!)
3 tsp. curry powder
1 (14.5-oz.) can Italian stewed tomatoes
½ cup chopped onions
1 cup chopped carrots
1 cup chopped zucchini
½ cup chopped celery
½ cup chopped bell pepper (green or red)
½ cup chopped apple (Trust me. It's delicious.)
1 cup cooked rice or quinoa (add 1 tsp. of chicken bouillon to your quinoa while it cooks)

> **HEALTH TIP:**
> Quinoa is higher in fiber than most grains. A better alternative to rice recipes would be to use quinoa.

1. Cook chicken with oil on medium heat for 7 minutes.

2. Add water, orange juice, bouillon, and curry powder to a large pot on medium heat. Squish the Italian stewed tomatoes (if there are large chunks) and place into pot.

3. Place chopped onion, carrots, zucchini, celery,

bell pepper, apple chunks, and cooked rice into pot. Shred chicken and place into pot.

4. Allow ingredients to simmer for about 15 minutes. Stir occasionally. When the carrots are slightly crunchy, turn down the heat and prepare to serve!

Also delicious with grilled cheese or cheese melted on a tortilla for dipping.

THAI RAMEN

If you still have ramen lying around, this is a great way to spice it up! You'll barely recognize the salty noodles other college students thrive on.

Star anise took me a while to find, but I uncovered it in an Asian market. If you don't visit these stores already, know this: you can get rice, noodles, Asian seasonings, and goodies like Pocky sticks and mochi on a college budget. If you still can't find or afford star anise, or aren't sure how often you'll use the little dried stars and so don't want to keep it on hand, it's okay to leave it out of this recipe.—Ashley

Makes 1 serving per package | Time: 5 minutes

2 cups water
1 package beef ramen noodles
1 dried star anise
½ cup ground or thinly sliced beef, optional
2 tsp. fish sauce
½ Tbsp. oil
1 tsp. minced garlic
2 tsp. sugar
½ tsp. lime juice
¼ tsp. sriracha or other hot sauce
chopped cilantro
lime wedge, optional

COOKING TIP:
This recipe doubles excellently. You can make as many packages of ramen as you need at a time!

1. In a saucepan over medium heat, heat oil and garlic, sautéing until fragrant, about 1–2 minutes. Add water, ramen seasoning, and star anise. Simmer for 3 minutes.

2. Add beef, ramen noodles, fish sauce, oil, garlic, sugar, lime juice, and hot sauce, and stir well. Simmer for 2 more minutes or until beef is done.

3. Remove star anise with a slotted spoon. Pour into serving bowl and top with chopped cilantro and lime wedge.

TOM KHA GAI (THAI CHICKEN COCONUT SOUP)

Looking for something completely different? Look no further than this Thai chicken coconut soup. It's both gluten- and dairy-free, making it a very accessible meal to serve to other people. This also doubles well, if you need to feed a lot of people.—Ashley

Makes 3–4 servings | Time: 30 minutes

3 cups chicken broth
1 cup coconut milk
1 stalk lemongrass, cut into 1½ inch pieces
2 slices galangal OR ginger
½ lb. boneless, skinless chicken breasts, thinly sliced
1 cup mushrooms
2 Tbsp. fish sauce
2 tsp. sugar
1 tsp. salt
lime slice, optional
chopped cilantro, optional

> **TIME-SAVING TIP:**
> Look for lemongrass and galangal at an Asian market.

1. In a large saucepan, bring broth, coconut milk, lemongrass, and galangal or ginger to a low boil. Simmer on low for 15–20 minutes.

2. Strain out galangal and lemongrass using a slotted spoon. Add chicken, mushrooms, fish sauce, sugar, and salt. Bring back to a low boil.

3. Simmer for 5 minutes or until chicken is done. Serve with a garnish of lime and cilantro.

LEMON SOUP

Chicken and a bit of spinach really round out this tangy soup. Crusty bread makes it a bit more filling if served as a full meal.—Ashley

Makes 5–6 servings | Time: 4 hours in a Crock-Pot

2 boneless skinless chicken breasts OR shredded cooked chicken
salt
pepper, freshly ground
4 cups chicken broth
1 cup shredded carrots
zest of 1 lemon
2 Tbsp. extra virgin olive oil
1 cup small pasta
4 sprigs dill
¾ cup spinach
1 lemon
½ cup feta cheese
crusty artisan bread, optional

DAIRY-FREE TIP:
To shorten the cook time to 15–20 minutes, cook in a large pot over medium-high heat and use shredded cooked chicken from another recipe (like Rosemary Chicken, page 101). Then add pasta and cook until done. Repeat the rest of the recipe as seen above. Also, to lengthen the time if you need to leave it for a long time, cook it in a Crock-Pot on low for 8 hours.

1. Season chicken on both sides with salt and pepper, and lay in the bottom of a large Crock-Pot. Combine chicken broth, carrots, lemon zest, and olive oil. Pour over chicken. Cook on high for 4 hours.

2. In the last 20 minutes of cooking, add the pasta and cook until done. Add dill and spinach. Stir or pull apart with forks to break up the chicken.

3. Cut lemon into wedges. Serve soup with feta cheese sprinkled on top, lemon wedges, and bread.

(with gluten-free pasta or rice)

HOMEMADE CHICKEN NOODLE SOUP

Save yourself the excess sodium and harmful preservatives by making chicken noodle soup from scratch. You'll give yourself a healthy meal without sacrificing a bit of that warm, healing taste.—Ashley

Makes 4–5 servings | Time: 40 minutes

¼ cup unsalted butter
1 medium yellow onion, diced
2 Tbsp. cornstarch OR ¼ cup flour
6 cups chicken broth
6–7 large fresh basil leaves OR 2 tsp. dried basil
1 tsp. minced or crushed garlic
salt and pepper to taste
2 boneless, skinless chicken breasts, cubed
1 Tbsp. olive oil
1 Tbsp. Montreal chicken seasoning
2 tsp. lemon juice
5 oz. noodles

1. Melt butter in a medium skillet. Add onion and cook until translucent. Add cornstarch to create a roux, stirring until creamy and lump-free. Transfer to a large pot.

2. Stir in chicken broth over medium-high heat. Add basil and garlic. Let simmer for 30 minutes.

3. Meanwhile, in a medium skillet, heat oil and add chicken. Scatter seasoning and lemon juice over meat and cook until juices run clear and chicken is done through. Add chicken to soup and continue simmering until 30 minutes are up.

4. Add noodles to the soup, and cook until done.

5. Alternately, make ahead by transferring roux and step 2 to a large slow cooker and allowing to simmer on medium for 3–5 hours. Add chicken once it's cooked. About half an hour from the finish, add noodles, and serve once they are soft.

(with gluten-free noodles)

CHEESE SOUP

The best way to eat cheddar is to have it as sharp as possible. Not everyone agrees with the taste of powerful cheeses; however, strong cheese like sharp cheddar will help flavor this soup well and keep it from tasting bland.—Ashley

Makes 4–6 servings | Time: 15 minutes

¼ cup butter
1 onion, chopped
2 Tbsp. cornstarch
3 cups chicken broth
3 cups milk
1 lb. sharp cheddar cheese, shredded
½ tsp. pepper

1. Melt butter in a large saucepan over medium heat, and add onion. Cook until translucent, and add flour. Stir continuously until there are no more lumps in the flour and the mixture is a warm golden brown.

2. Pour in chicken broth, stirring until well combined and the mixture has slightly thickened. Add milk and raise heat, bringing the mixture to a boil. Remove from heat.

3. Add shredded cheese about 1 cup at a time, stirring until completely melted and incorporated into the soup. If the cheese is not melting, return saucepan back to very low heat and stir. You may want a stronger-tasting soup, and if you have any extra cheese, add that to taste. Season with pepper.

Variations: To make the soup heartier, add cooked ground beef or chopped bacon, diced tomatoes, a sprinkle of your favorite dried herbs (like oregano, rosemary, or basil), and serve over rice.

TOMATO SOUP

While it's possible to make soup out of a can, it's often bland and uninteresting. If you have the time to make your own, your taste buds will thank you!—Ashley

Makes 4–6 servings | Time: 5 minutes

1 (10.75-oz.) can condensed tomato soup
2 cups chicken broth
½ tsp. onion powder
½ Tbsp. Italian seasoning
¼ tsp. salt
¼ tsp. pepper

1. Heat a saucepan over medium heat, and combine all ingredients. Bring to a simmer and cook until heated through. Serve warm.

 DINNER

You may have noticed that we have loads more dinner options than just about anything else. You see, we understand how pressed for time college students are. And though time is precious and food is important, you will probably have more time to make dinners than any other time during the day. Obviously everyone's schedule is different, but we've found it to be most useful to make larger meals for dinner, so that we could enjoy the leftovers for lunch or dinner for several days.

PAPRIKA BROWN SUGAR CHICKEN

This sweet chicken is a breeze to make and so yummy to eat. Eat it alongside mashed potatoes, Sweet Potato Chips (page 183) or in a salad (Sweet Garden Salad, page 75).—Chelsea

Makes 2–3 servings | Time: 40 minutes
(I recommend marinating the night before)

2 large boneless, skinless chicken breasts
¼ cup brown sugar
1½ Tbsp. paprika
½ Tbsp. chili powder
1 tsp. oregano
1 tsp. garlic powder
1 Tbsp. oil
pepper for extra taste

1. Combine brown sugar, paprika, chili powder, oregano, and garlic powder into a large plastic bag.

2. Slice chicken into strips and drop them into the plastic bag. Squish bag to mix chicken with seasonings. Place bag in fridge for 30 minutes to marinate (though more time will just make it more yummy!).

3. Add oil to a pan and cook chicken on high heat for 10 minutes or until cooked. Sprinkle with pepper for extra flavoring.

Variation: You can also use the same marinade for 1 lb. fish.

(if you marinate the night before)

ROSEMARY LEMON CHICKEN

This savory and juicy chicken is great by itself, or as part of other recipes as a way to use up leftovers.—Ashley

Makes 2–3 servings | Time: 20 minutes

3 Tbsp. extra-virgin olive oil
2 boneless, skinless chicken breasts, cut into large chunks
1 Tbsp. grill seasoning (e.g. Montreal Seasoning) OR coarse
    salt and black pepper
6 cloves garlic, crushed
3 Tbsp. fresh rosemary leaves OR 1 Tbsp. dried rosemary
1 lemon, zested and juiced
½ cup chicken broth

1. Heat oil in a medium skillet, and add chicken. Season on both sides with seasoning or salt and pepper, garlic, rosemary, and lemon zest.

2. Cook chicken until just done, 12–15 minutes. Turn off the heat but leave on the stove burner. Add the lemon juice and chicken broth, and leave for about 5 minutes.

3. Remove from heat and serve with pan juices spooned over the chicken.

SLOW COOKER CILANTRO LIME CHICKEN

This is a great set-and-forget meal! After hours of cooking, the chicken just falls apart when cut. Make sure you pick your salsa carefully for the right level of spiciness.—Ashley

Makes 4–5 servings | Time: 2–3 OR 4–6 hours

1 (24-oz.) can salsa
¼ cup chopped cilantro
1 package taco seasoning
1 Tbsp. lime juice
1 small can green chiles
4 boneless, skinless chicken breasts

1. In a bowl, mix together salsa, cilantro, taco seasoning, lime juice, and chiles. Lay chicken breasts in the bottom of a slow cooker and smother with salsa mixture.

2. Cook on low for 4–6 hours, or on high for 2–3 until chicken is done through.

SALT AND PEPPER PORK

This is a super fast, healthy, and delicious main course to impress a date without the stress of slaving in the kitchen all day. Mashed potatoes, Speedy BBQ Baked Beans (page 184), Sweet Potato Chips (page 183), or a salad are fantastic sides.—Chelsea

Makes 2–3 servings | Time: 20 minutes

2 Tbsp. oil, divided
1 red bell pepper, thinly sliced
1 green bell pepper, thinly sliced
1 yellow or orange bell pepper, thinly sliced
salt and pepper
1 lb. pork chops (preferably boneless)

Please do step 1 and 2 together.

1. Add 1 tablespoon oil to pan on medium-high heat and then add all three bell peppers. Sauté for about ten minutes or until slightly blackened.

2. Add 1 tablespoon of oil to separate pan on medium-high heat. Salt and pepper both sides of each pork chop then add to pan. Cook each side for five minutes then remove.

3. Serve sautéed bell peppers on top of the cooked pork chops.

MOM'S BBQ CUPS

This is a family tradition that will be a huge hit with roommates, family, and friends! These cups are easy for the grab-and-go student.—Chelsea

Makes 21 muffin-sized cups | Time: 1 hour

2 loaves Rhodes frozen dough (follow instructions on package to thaw and rise dough) or Gluten-Free Bread for Mom's Cups (page 195).
2 lb. lean ground beef
2 cloves garlic, minced
1 red pepper, diced
½ large onion, diced
½ medium zucchini, diced
2½ cups BBQ Sauce
2½ cups shredded Colby Jack cheese

1. Preheat oven to 350 degrees. Oil two cupcake pans.
2. Brown ground beef in a pan and drain fat. Add minced garlic, diced red peppers, onion, and zucchini on medium heat. Cook for 5 minutes. Then add BBQ sauce.
3. Flour your hands then grab a small handful of dough. Pat dough into a flat circle just a little bigger than your palm. Gently press dough into muffin cup. Repeat until 21 cupcake cups are filled.
4. Place a couple spoonfuls of BBQ beef in each cup. Cover with cheese.

5. Bake in oven for 18 minutes or until dough begins to slightly brown.

6. Dip in additional BBQ sauce or ketchup.

(with gluten-free dough)

CHICKEN FRIED RICE

This is a quick and easy Asian recipe that makes a lot of food for very little effort. In order to have amazing fried rice, cook rice the day before. Use a bit less water than the instructions on the bag call for. Hard rice fries better.—Chelsea

Makes 4–5 servings | Time: 30 minutes

5 Tbsp. oil, divided

2 large boneless, skinless chicken breasts, diced

4 cups cooked rice

2 Tbsp. soy sauce

½ Tbsp. chili garlic sauce (Asian section of grocery store)

2 eggs

2 cups frozen veggie mix

1. Pour 1 tablespoon of oil in pan and add diced chicken. Cook on high for about 7 minutes.

2. In a separate pan add 2 tablespoons of oil with 4 cups of rice on high heat. Stir together for 5 minutes.

3. Mix the soy sauce and chili garlic sauce in a small bowl then add to rice pan. If rice begins to stick to the bottom of the pan, add 1 more tablespoon of oil. Mix well until rice is a light brown then add the cooked chicken.

4. Add 1 tablespoon of oil and the frozen veggies to the chicken. Stir until thawed.

5. Crack two eggs into pan with veggies, mix until eggs are scrambled.

6. Add veggie/egg mixture into rice pan and mix together.

(with gluten-free
soy sauce)

SPAGHETTI PIE

Here is a simpler way to get the taste of lasagna without the extra effort and time.—Chelsea

Makes 8 servings | Time: 50 minutes

1 (16-oz.) package macaroni or penne noodles
1 lb. lean ground beef
2 (24-oz.) jars spaghetti sauce

1 cup ricotta cheese
3 eggs
1 Tbsp. Italian seasoning
2 cups shredded cheese

1 cup chopped zucchini
1 cup chopped mushrooms
1 cup chopped bell pepper (any color)
1 cup chopped sweet onion

1. Preheat oven to 375 degrees.
2. Start noodles on the stove. Follow package directions.
3. Brown ground beef on medium-high heat. Drain most of the fat then add veggies. Cook for another 3 minutes and then add ½ jar spaghetti sauce and Italian stewed tomatoes.
4. Once noodles are done, strain water and add noodles to a 9 x 13 dish. Mix Ricotta cheese, eggs, remaining ½ jar spaghetti sauce, and Italian seasoning in another bowl. Pour mixture over noodles and mix well.
5. Distribute spaghetti sauce mix evenly on top of noodles. Place in oven for 20 minutes.

6. At 20 minutes, sprinkle shredded cheese on top and return to oven for another 15 minutes. Then pull out and serve!

(with gluten-
free noodles)

SHEPHERD'S PIE

Here is a hardy American dish that will remind you of home and those delicious meals your mom could whip up like a pro.—Chelsea

Makes 6–7 servings | Time: 30 minutes

1 lb. lean ground beef
1 Tbsp. oil
1 clove garlic, minced
½ cup diced sweet onion
2 cups mixed veggies, thawed
1 (14.5-oz.) can Italian stewed tomatoes, squished
¼ cup tomato paste
1 tsp. dried basil
8 servings or 4 cups boxed mashed potatoes (which normally includes butter and milk)
1 egg, beaten
2 cups shredded cheese

1. Preheat oven to 350 degrees.

2. Brown ground beef in a pan on medium-high heat. Drain fat and put ground beef in a bowl.

3. Heat oil in pan and add garlic and onion. Cook for 3 minutes and then stir in mixed veggies and cook for another 3 minutes.

4. Add squished Italian stewed tomatoes, tomato paste, basil, and ground beef into pan and mix well. Place all contents in a 9 x 13 baking dish.

5. Follow instructions on mashed potato box for 8 servings (4 cups) of mashed potatoes but also add egg into mashed potato.

6. Spread mashed potatoes over meat mixture. Top with cheese.

7. Place in the oven for 15 minutes then pull it out and enjoy!

HOMEMADE TOMATO SAUCE

It's possible to buy tomato sauce at the store, but you may not get much out of it, or it may not taste as good as it should for the price. Store this in airtight mason jars to save money, a trip to the store, and stress! This recipe comes courtesy of my friend Hannah Dunaway.—Ashley

Makes about 5 cups | Time: 35 minutes

1 lb. ground beef
½ chopped onion
2 cloves garlic
1 Tbsp. olive oil
½ Tbsp. basil
½ Tbsp. rosemary
parsley, to taste
oregano, to taste
italian seasoning, to taste
1 pinch cinnamon, optional
1 (28-oz.) can spaghetti sauce
2 (8-oz.) cans tomato sauce
6 oz. tomato paste
2 cubes (2 tsp.) beef bouillon

1. Brown the ground beef in a large skillet. Add onion, garlic, olive oil, and seasonings, and sauté until onion is soft and translucent.

2. Pour in sauces and paste and stir well. Drop in

bouillon and stir until dissolved. Allow to cook down over medium-high heat, about 30 minutes. Cooking longer over lower heat will get it thicker, if desired.

CHICKEN PICCATA

This is far and away one of my favorites! I learned to make it because the restaurants I ordered it from never served quite enough, which should tell you how much I love it. You can use the salty capers for an authentic look and taste, but if it's not in your budget or fridge space, this meal is delicious enough without it!

If you do opt for capers, you can find them in your local grocery. They look a little bit like dark green peas and come in a jar.—Ashley

Makes 3–4 servings | Time: 20 minutes

¼ cup flour OR 2 Tbsp. cornstarch
salt and pepper, to taste
2 chicken breasts, butterflied*
4 Tbsp. unsalted butter
⅓ cup lemon juice
½ cup chicken broth
brined capers, optional

1. In a shallow bowl big enough to hold the chicken, mix flour, salt, and pepper. Coat chicken in flour mixture and remove.

2. Heat butter in a large nonstick skillet over medium-high heat. Add chicken in a single layer. Cook about 6 minutes on each side or until chicken is done. Remove from skillet. Set aside; keep warm.

3. Add lemon juice, chicken broth, and capers to skillet, scraping the bottom to loosen brown bits from cooking. Simmer until thickened (yields about ¼ cup sauce or so). If necessary, add more salt and pepper to taste.

4. Remove from heat. Spoon sauce over chicken, and serve over angel hair or fettuccine pasta.

To butterfly chicken breasts: lay the chicken breast flat on a cutting board. Usually, there is a piece of meat (the tender) that sticks out from the rest, connected by bits of tissue. Cut away tender and store it for another recipe (e.g. Coconut Chicken Strips, page 56). Working parallel to the cutting board, slice chicken breast almost all the way through lengthwise, and open up the chicken breast so it looks a bit like a butterfly. Place into a gallon-sized plastic bag and seal tightly. Using a meat tenderizer or a rolling pin, gently pound the chicken until it's roughly the same thickness throughout.

(with cornstarch)

CHICKEN PARMESAN

Making this Italian favorite at home saves money, and time—if you consider the time it takes to go to an Italian restaurant and have it made for you. You can eat this on its own, or serve it over pasta noodles to round out the meal.—Ashley

Makes 2 servings | Time: 15 minutes

½ cup flour
1 egg
Panko crumbs
2 chicken breasts, butterflied*
salt and pepper, to taste
1 Tbsp. extra-virgin olive oil
1½ cup tomato sauce (marinara works well here)
sliced mozzarella cheese
parmesan cheese, to taste

GLUTEN-FREE TIP:
For a gluten-free option, place about 1½ cups of rice cereal in a food processor. Blend until finely ground into crumbs.

1. Preheat oven to 400 degrees. Set up an assembly line of bowls: flour, egg, and panko crumbs.
2. Season chicken on both sides with salt and pepper. Dredge each breast in flour, then dip in egg, and then dredge on both sides in the bread crumbs.
3. Heat oil in a large skillet until almost smoking. Cook chicken until golden brown on each side, about 2 minutes per side.
4. Transfer chicken to a baking dish or sheet. Top each with tomato sauce and cheeses. Bake until chicken is cooked through and cheese has melted, about 5–7 minutes. Remove and serve with additional sauce.

To butterfly chicken breasts: lay the chicken breast flat on a cutting board. Usually, there is a piece of meat (the tender) that sticks out from the rest, connected by bits of tissue. Cut away tender and store it for another recipe. Working parallel to the cutting board, slice chicken breast almost all the way through lengthwise, and open up the chicken breast so it looks a bit like a butterfly. Place into a gallon-sized plastic bag and seal tightly. Using a meat tenderizer or a rolling pin, gently pound the chicken until it's roughly the same thickness throughout.

(without cheese)   (with gluten-free
                           breadcrumbs)

CREAM CHEESE CHICKEN AND RICE CHILI

This is a memorable rice dish to impress your roommates and make them drool. It's also a hearty meal and great for leftovers!—Chelsea

Makes 6–7 servings | Time: 3.5 hours

1 (10-oz.) can Rotel tomatoes with green chilies (if you don't like spice, just use Rotel tomatoes without chilies)
1 (15.25-oz.) can corn, undrained
1 (15-oz.) can black beans, drained and rinsed
1 package ranch dressing mix
1 Tbsp. cumin
1 tsp. chili powder
1 tsp. onion powder
1 (8-oz.) package cream cheese
2 large boneless, skinless chicken breasts, diced
4 cups cooked rice

1. Turn Crock-Pot on high then add Rotel tomatoes, corn, black beans, package of ranch dressing mix, cumin, chili powder, and onion powder. Break cream cheese in pieces and mix everything together in Crock-Pot.
2. Add chicken to Crock-Pot and cook chili for 3.5 hours on high. Then stir and check chicken.
3. Once both rice and chili are done, serve chili over rice. It's delicious!

CREAM CHEESE CHICKEN PASTA

This slightly spicy but incredible creamy homemade sauce is the perfect addition to your collection of fun, quick pasta dishes. If you don't like spice, add less red pepper flakes.—Chelsea

Makes 4–5 servings | Time: 30 minutes

1 (16-oz.) package penne noodles
2 boneless, skinless chicken breasts, diced
2 Tbsp. oil
1 garlic clove, minced
1 cup diced onion
1 cup sliced mushrooms
1 cup sliced yellow squash
¼ tsp. black pepper

1 (14.5 oz.) can Italian stewed tomatoes, squished
½ tsp. dried oregano
½ tsp. dried basil
½-1 tsp. red pepper flakes (depending on how spicy you want it)
2 Tbsp. tomato paste
½ cup water
3 oz. cream cheese
¼ cup shredded cheese (cheddar or mozzarella)
3 oz. baby spinach
parmesan cheese to sprinkle

1. Boil a large pot of water on high heat. Add penne noodles and cook until noodles are soft (about ten minutes). Drain pasta and rinse in cold water.
2. Add 1 tablespoon of oil to pot along with diced

chicken. Cook on medium high for 7 minutes. Drain excess water.

3. Add another tablespoon of oil, garlic, onion, mushrooms, and yellow squash. Sauté for 3 minutes.

4. Turn heat to medium. Add the Italian stewed tomatoes (undrained!), oregano, basil, red pepper flakes, tomato paste, and water. Cut cream cheese into chunks and add to pot with shredded cheese. Stir until creamy.

5. Add spinach and stir until spinach is cooked then include noodles and mix ingredients together.

6. Sprinkle with parmesan cheese to individual bowls.

(gluten-free noodles)

Gluten-free noodles do not keep in the fridge as well as normal noodles.

CAJUN CHICKEN ALFREDO

My mom, the best chef I know, perfected this creamy, slightly spicy twist on an Italian classic. The sauce is made from scratch, and so it tastes better than any I've gotten from a store. You can adjust the Cajun seasoning to your taste if you want it spicier or more mild.—Ashley

Makes 4 servings | Time: 25 minutes

3 lbs. boneless, skinless chicken breasts

1 Tbsp. Cajun spice

2 Tbsp. butter

1 medium onion

1½ cups milk

1½ cups cream

1 Tbsp. flour OR ½ Tbsp. cornstarch

2 tsp. dried basil

2 Tbsp. chopped sun-dried tomatoes

¼ tsp. salt

1 tsp. pepper

1 tsp. garlic powder

¼ cup grated parmesan cheese

4 servings cooked linguine

1. Cube chicken, and toss in Cajun seasoning. Set aside.

2. In a large skillet, melt butter and sauté onion until just transparent. Add chicken and sauté until tender, about 5–7 minutes.

3. Reduce heat, and add milk, cream, tomatoes, and spices. Heat through.

4. Serve over hot linguine and toss with parmesan.

(with cornstarch and
gluten-free pasta)

BAKED PESTO CHICKEN

If you want to impress your date with your cooking skills, give this recipe a try. It's super simple to make but tastes like you went to a fancy Italian restaurant. This open-faced chicken dish will leave you humming with the sun-dried tomato and pesto flavoring.—Chelsea

Makes 4 servings | Time: 45 Minutes

2 large boneless, skinless chicken breasts
2 Tbsp. pesto
¼ cup sun-dried tomatoes
2 handfuls spinach
½ cup mozzarella cheese
grated parmesan cheese to sprinkle
½ tsp. black pepper

1. Preheat oven to 350 degrees.
2. Slice chicken breast in half horizontally and place in a small or medium glass pan.
3. Spread pesto and sprinkle sun-dried tomatoes over all four slices. Add spinach and sprinkle mozzarella cheese, parmesan cheese, and black pepper on top.
4. Cover pan with aluminium foil and place in the oven for 30–40 minutes. Make sure chicken looks white when sliced.

(without cheese)

PESTO AND PARMESAN STUFFED CHICKEN

Filling chicken with delicious pesto and parmesan makes this an interesting spin on what started out as chicken cordon bleu. It makes the chicken savory and flavorful, and great for showing off without the effort!—Ashley

Makes 4 servings | Time: 40 minutes

4 boneless, skinless chicken breasts
4 Tbsp. pesto
1 Tbsp. lemon juice
¼ cup sour cream
¼ cup grated mozzarella
¼ cup grated parmesan cheese
½ cup panko or bread crumbs
2 eggs, beaten
salt and pepper, to taste

GLUTEN-FREE TIP:
For a gluten-free option, place about 1½ cups of rice cereal or other gluten-free cereal in a food processor. Blend until finely ground into crumbs.

1. Preheat oven to 375 degrees. Place chicken in a gallon-sized bag, and using a meat tenderizer or rolling pin, pound until chicken is very flat. Set aside. Lightly grease a casserole dish, and set aside as well.

2. In a bowl, mix pesto, lemon juice, sour cream, and mozzarella cheese. Divide and spread even portions of pesto mixture over each chicken breast, keeping it about ½ inch from the edge of chicken. Roll chicken breasts and pin them shut with toothpicks.

3. Mix panko and parmesan in a bowl, and prepare a second bowl with the beaten eggs. Dip each chicken breast into egg mixture, and let excess drip off. Then dip into panko mixture, and set into prepared casserole dish.

4. Bake for 30–35 minutes until chicken is firm and golden brown. Serve hot.

CARAMELIZED HAM AND CHEESE ROLLS

Here is a fun summer recipe that is perfect with Speedy BBQ Baked Beans (page 184), Sweet Potato Chips (page 183), or Italian Noodle Salad (page 181) .—Chelsea

Makes 15 rolls | Time: about 1 hour

Don't shy away because of the dough recipe. It is sooo easy!

Dough
3 tsp. yeast
2¼ cup warm water
1 Tbsp. brown sugar
3 eggs
4½–5 cups flour
2 tsp. salt

1. Mix brown sugar and yeast in warm (120 degrees) water in a bowl and leave for five minutes.
2. Add eggs, flour, and salt to a large bowl. Mix wet and dry ingredients together with your hand until dough is sticky. (Cooking Tip: this dough was originally made with gluten-free flour that LOVES to soak up water. If you use normal flour, you may need to add extra.)
3. For best results, allow the dough to rise in a glass bowl for 20 minutes in the oven on warm. Cover with a damp rag so dough keeps its moisture.

1 lb. deli ham, thinly sliced
12 slices Swiss cheese, thinly sliced

Glaze
8 Tbsp. butter
2 Tbsp. brown sugar
1 Tbsp. Worcestershire sauce
1 Tbsp. Dijon mustard
½ Tbsp. poppy seeds

1. Preheat oven to 350 degrees and coat a cookie sheet with cooking spray or oil.
2. Lay two strips of plastic wrap (about 18 inches each) on the table and then sprinkle with flour. Use a rolling pin to flatten out a square in dough on top of plastic wrap.
3. Evenly space out slices of Swiss cheese on top of dough and place ham slices on top.
4. Use plastic wrap to take right side of dough and roll it towards the left side as you would with cinnamon rolls.
5. Slice 15 evenly measured pieces and place in pan. (Floss works great for this!)
6. Melt butter in microwave. Add brown sugar, Worcestershire sauce, Dijon mustard, and poppy seeds. Drizzle glaze over each roll.
7. Bake rolls for 25 minutes or until rolls begin to turn golden.

BUFFALO CHICKEN ROLL

Enjoy this roll stuffed with oozing buffalo sauce, chicken, some tasty veggies, and cheese. I recommend partnering this recipe with a salad or Speedy BBQ Baked Beans (page 184)!—Chelsea

Makes 4–5 servings | Time: 45 minutes

Follow the recipe Gluten-Free Bread for Mom's Cups (page 195) for the appropriate amount of dough, or use about 2 loaves of Rhodes dough from the freezer section of the grocery store. Follow instructions on package to thaw and rise dough.

2 large chicken breasts, diced
1 Tbsp. oil
⅓ cup ranch dressing
½ cup Frank's Red Hot Wings sauce
3 cups shredded mozzarella, divided
½ red onion, diced
½ green pepper, diced
1 egg white
poppy seeds to sprinkle

1. Preheat oven to 425 degrees.
2. In a pan, cook chicken in oil on medium-high heat for about 7 minutes.
3. Add flour to table and roll out dough in a rectangle, about ¼ inch thick. Mix ranch and Frank's sauce in a bowl then spread over dough (like you're making pizza). Sprinkle two cups mozzarella cheese over spread. Then add chicken, onions, green peppers, and the last cup cheese.
4. Slowly roll your dough (like cinnamon rolls), cut in

half, and place on an oiled pan. Slather the top with egg white and sprinkle with poppy seeds.

5. Bake in oven for 20–25 minutes or until slightly brown.

6. Slice and enjoy. I dip my slices in ranch.

(with gluten-free dough and flour)

BAKED POTATOES AND CHILI

Sometimes we just need something tasty and hearty. This meal is fantastic for lots of people or lots of leftovers. Freeze in portion-sized baggies for future hectic days.—Chelsea

Makes 6–7 servings | Time: 50 minutes

2½–3 lb. small red potatoes
2 boneless, skinless chicken breasts, diced
1 Tbsp. oil
5 cups salsa
1 (15-oz.) can black beans, rinsed and drained
1 (15.25-oz.) can kidney beans, rinsed and drained

Toppings:
4 green onions, thinly sliced rounds
sour cream
shredded cheese

1. Preheat oven to 400 degrees.
2. Rinse potatoes and cut in fourths. Place them on a cookie sheet and put it in the oven for 35–45 minutes.
3. Cook chicken in a pan on medium-high heat for 7–8 minutes with oil.
4. Add salsa, beans, and chicken to a pot and turn on medium-low until potatoes are done.
5. Once you can easily cut through the potatoes, add some potatoes to the bottom of a bowl, smother them with your chicken chili and add green onions, sour cream, and cheese.

(without cheese and
sour cream)

HAWAIIAN HAYSTACKS

This recipe is a burst of delicious flavors from pineapple to mushrooms over a creamy sauce and rice. It's quick (how fast can you cut!?) and simple to make. Sprinkle with cheese and enjoy with friends!—Chelsea

Makes 5–6 servings | Time: 35–40 minutes

3 cups uncooked rice

2 (18-oz.) cans Progresso Creamy Mushroom soup

3 Tbsp. sour cream

1 (12.5-oz.) can chicken or cook 1 large boneless, skinless chicken breast, diced

1 cup chopped sweet onions

1 cup thinly sliced celery

1 cup diced tomatoes

1 cup chopped carrots

1 cup diced bell pepper (any color)

1 cup diced mushrooms

1 cup cheese

1 can mandarin oranges

1 can pineapple tidbits

TIME-SAVING TIP:
I highly recommend getting a rice cooker.

1. Start 3 cups of uncooked rice according to package.

2. Add soup, sour cream, and chicken to a saucepan on medium heat. Stir occasionally.

3. Once rice is done, add rice, sauce, and then

whatever ingredients you want to a bowl and sprinkle with cheese.

(minus toppings)   (with gluten-free creamy
                      mushroom soup)

TUNA FISH CASSEROLE

This is a quick recipe to toss in the oven and devour! I also recommend freezing it in small baggies so you can eat it during days when you barely have time to breathe, let alone cook something. Great with a side salad.—Chelsea

Makes 6–7 servings | Time: 35 minutes

1 (12-oz.) package rotini pasta noodles
2 (5-oz.) cans tuna
2 (18-oz.) cans Progresso Creamy Mushroom soup
⅓ cup sour cream
1 cup frozen peas, thawed in hot water
1 cup thinly sliced celery
2 cups shredded cheese

1. Preheat oven to 350 degrees.
2. Cook pasta according to directions on box.
3. Mix tuna, soup, sour cream, peas, and celery in a 9 x 13 pan. Once noodles are done, mix noodles in also. Place pan in oven for 20 minutes.
4. Remove pan and add cheese. Bake for an additional 5 minutes.

(with gluten-free noodles and
creamy mushroom soup)

CHICKEN CORDON BLEU CASSEROLE

It's time to take this gourmet meal and make it easy! Perfect for a fancy date!—Chelsea

Makes 6–7 servings | Time: 1 hour

Casserole

3 large boneless, skinless chicken breasts
1 lb. honey ham, sliced
9 slices Swiss cheese, thinly sliced

Sauce

4 Tbsp. butter
2 (14-oz.) cans evaporated milk
¼ cup almond milk
2 Tbsp. lemon juice
4 Tbsp. flour
1 Tbsp. Dijon mustard
½ tsp. paprika
¼ tsp. pepper

HEALTH TIP:
To make this recipe healthier, use coconut oil instead of butter and almond milk instead of evaporated milk. Add 1 tsp. of chicken bouillon to sauce if using almond milk.

Topping

1½ cups breadcrumbs
1½ tsp. crushed dried parsley
pepper, optional

1. Preheat oven to 350 degrees. Lightly butter a 9 x 13 pan.

2. Cut chicken in small pieces and cook on the stove on medium heat for 7–8 minutes. Place chicken evenly on the bottom of the 9 x 13 pan.

3.　　Rip ham in chunks and distribute evenly over the chicken. Place Swiss cheese on top.

4.　Melt butter in microwave in a medium-sized bowl. Add evaporated milk, almond milk, lemon juice, flour, Dijon mustard, paprika, and pepper, and stir together. Drizzle sauce over cheese.

5.　Sprinkle bread crumbs over the sauce then spread parsley. Add pepper for extra taste.

6.　Bake for 45 minutes or until casserole begins to bubble. Allow casserole to cool for around 10 minutes and then serve.

(with gluten-free bread-
crumbs and flour)

CORNBREAD CHILI CASSEROLE

Cornbread and chili are classics, so why not place them together in a casserole? This is a fantastic freezer meal or it's ideal for leftovers that last the whole week when you are too busy to cook more than once.—Chelsea

Makes 6–8 servings | Time: 45 minutes

1 (12-oz.) box cornbread mix (and other necessary ingredients listed on the box)
2 boneless, skinless chicken breasts, diced
1 Tbsp. oil
2 cups mild or medium salsa
1 can kidney beans
2 Tbsp. honey
1 tsp. oregano
1½ cups shredded cheese

1. Preheat oven to 350 degrees.
2. Make cornbread mix and set aside.
3. On medium-high heat, cook diced chicken in oil for 7–8 minutes.
4. In a 9 x 13 pan, mix salsa, kidney beans, honey, oregano, and cooked chicken.
5. Spread cornbread mix evenly on top. Bake for 30–35 minutes or until top is golden.
6. Take it out and cover top with cheese and return it to the oven for another 2–3 minutes.

(with gluten-free cornbread)

GREEN PEPPER MEATLOAF

Not only are these small meatloaf patties fun and delicious to eat as meatloaf, they are also perfect for hamburgers! Try with Italian Garlic Potatoes (page 180), mashed potatoes, or a salad.—Chelsea

Makes about 9 patties | Time: 45 minutes

2 green bell peppers
1 lb. lean ground beef
½ yellow onion, diced
½ cup quick oats
½ cup ketchup
½ cup tomato paste
2 cloves garlic, minced
salt and black pepper to sprinkle
1–1½ cups BBQ sauce
1–1½ cups shredded cheese

1. Preheat oven to 400 degrees.
2. Cut green peppers horizontally into ¼-inch rings and remove the seeds. Do not use ends. Put those in your eggs in the morning.
3. Place pepper slices evenly apart on a cookie sheet.
4. Mix ground beef, onion, quick oats, ketchup, tomato paste, garlic, and salt and pepper in a bowl. Spoon meat mixture into the center of each green pepper slice.
5. Bake for 30 minutes. Check to make sure meat is not pink.

6. Take out and add a spoonful of BBQ sauce and some cheese to the top of every patty. Melt in oven for 1 minute.

(without cheese)   (with gluten-free quick oats)

CHEESEBURGER ZUCCHINI BOATS

Are you craving your favorite cheeseburger but trying to stay away from the calories? Here is the solution. These cheeseburger-packed zucchini boats drizzled with ketchup and mustard will hush your craving and satisfy your taste buds!—Chelsea

Makes 8 boats | Time: 1 hour

4 medium-large zucchini
1 lb. extra-lean ground beef
1 garlic clove, minced
½ small red onion, diced
1 (6-oz.) can tomato paste
¼ cup water
1 Tbsp. yellow mustard
½ tsp. salt
½ tsp. parsley
½ cup shredded sharp cheddar cheese

Toppings
dill pickles (chips)
ketchup
yellow mustard

1. Preheat oven to 400 degrees and oil a cookie sheet.
2. Wash zucchini, cut off stems, and cut in half horizontally. Scoop out center until each zucchini is only ¼ inch thick. Save ½ cup of the insides and chop it up.
3. Brown hamburger in pan and drain fat then add garlic and onion. Sauté for 2 minutes.
4. Add chopped zucchini, tomato paste, water, yellow

mustard, salt, and parsley to the pan. Stir to combine.

5. Place zucchini on cookie sheet and fill with meat mixture.

6. Cover with cheese and bake for 35 minutes.

7. Add a layer of pickles, then drizzle ketchup and mustard over the top.

(without cheese)

TWO CHEESE ALFREDO PIZZA

This thin homemade crust smothered in alfredo sauce and cheese will turn into a quick weekend tradition.—Chelsea

Makes 1 large pizza (the size of a cookie sheet)
Time: 45 minutes

Crust
1 Tbsp. yeast
1⅓ cups very warm water (about 120 degrees)
2 tsp. brown sugar
3–4 cups flour
6 Tbsp. oil (recommend avocado oil)
1 tsp. salt

Toppings
1 large boneless, skinless chicken breast, diced
1 Tbsp. oil
1 (15-oz.) jar alfredo sauce
2½ cups shredded mozzarella cheese, divided
1 cup diced yellow squash
1 cup diced mushrooms
½ cup diced sun-dried tomatoes
Grated parmesan cheese to sprinkle

1. Preheat oven to 425 degrees.
2. Add all ingredients for crust into a bowl and mix with your hands. Add extra flour if needed. Dough should be slightly sticky.
3. Oil a cookie sheet and spread dough evenly over sheet with floured hands.
4. Place in oven for 10 minutes.
5. Cook chicken in oil on medium heat for 7–8 minutes or until cooked.

6. Spread alfredo sauce evenly over pizza crust. Sprinkle with 1½ cup of mozzarella cheese, yellow squash, mushrooms, sun-dried tomatoes, chicken, and then add remaining mozzarella cheese. Sprinkle with parmesan cheese.

7. Bake pizza for 15 minutes or until edges are a light brown.

8. Allow pizza to cool for 5 minutes and then slice and serve.

(with gluten free flour; check alfredo sauce for flour as a thickening agent)

CAPRESE PIZZA

This is a very light, tasty pizza, similar to the classic margherita. It's a great break from heavier pizzas, though no less delicious—Ashley

Makes 3–4 servings | Time: 25 minutes

1 pizza crust
olive oil
sliced fresh mozzarella
about 10 large basil leaves, julienned
2 tomatoes, thinly sliced
Balsamic Vinegar Reduction (page 79)

> **COOKING TIP:**
> Go to your local grocery store, and ask the bakery if they sell raw bread dough. Thaw this and use it as your pizza crust, stretching out to a circle and brushing with olive oil before topping. This is much better than dry store-bought crust!

1. Preheat oven to 425 degrees. Place pizza crust on a baking sheet and brush lightly with olive oil. Top with mozzarella, basil, and tomatoes. Bake 15–20 minutes or until pizza dough is golden brown and cheese has melted.

2. Drizzle balsamic reduction over the pizza. Slice and serve.

(with goat or feta cheese)

MOZZARELLA, BASIL, PEACH, AND BALSAMIC PIZZA

Some time ago, I came across this oddly delicious pizza combination, and decided I had to make it myself! It perfectly combines fruity, tart, and savory in one pizza. Try it to shake up the usual toppings you can get from any freezer aisle.—Ashley

Makes 3–4 servings | Time: 25 minutes

1 pizza crust
olive oil
sliced fresh mozzarella
2 peaches, sliced
5 large basil leaves
Balsamic Vinegar Reduction (page 79)

> **COOKING TIP:**
> Go to your local grocery store, and ask the bakery if they sell raw bread dough. Thaw this and use it as your pizza crust, stretching out to a circle and brushing with olive oil before topping. This is much better than dry store-bought crust!

1. Preheat oven to 425 degrees. Place pizza crust on a baking sheet and brush lightly with olive oil. Top with mozzarella, peaches, and basil leaves. Bake in the oven for 15–20 minutes or until pizza dough is golden brown and cheese has melted.

2. Drizzle balsamic reduction over the pizza. Slice and serve.

(with goat or feta cheese)

PIZZA BOMBS

If you need some pizza flavor for a party but don't want to break the bank, give these a shot! They're gooey and delicious. Eat them all yourself or serve as a side.—Ashley

Makes 16 bombs | Time: 25 minutes

1 tube biscuit dough
8 sticks mozzarella string cheese OR 6 oz. low-moisture
    mozzarella
16 slices pepperoni or salami
1 Tbsp. olive oil
¼ cup parmesan cheese
Italian seasoning

1. Preheat oven to 400 degrees.
2. Split each of the biscuits in half so that you have 16 discs. Divide cheese into 16 pieces.
3. Place cheese and pepperoni on each disc, and wrap dough around it to form a ball. Set each on a baking dish, about 2 inches apart.
4. Brush each ball with olive oil and sprinkle with both cheese and Italian seasoning. Bake until golden brown, 10–15 minutes. Serve immediately.

ITALIAN ZUCCHINI BOATS

Craving something Italian but tired of spaghetti? Try these zucchini boats smothered in a delicious meaty saucy and plenty of cheese! It's a quick and healthy recipe you will love.—Chelsea

Makes 10 zucchini boats | Time: 30 minutes

1 lb. ground beef
1 small onion, diced
1 (24-oz.) jar spaghetti sauce
5 zucchinis
2 cups shredded cheese
Italian seasoning and pepper for taste

1. Preheat oven to 400 degrees.
2. Brown ground beef, drain fat, and add onion. Cook on medium for 2 minutes or until onions look transparent. Add spaghetti sauce and turn off heat.
3. Cut zucchinis in half horizontally. Use a spoon to scrape out middle contents.
4. Place zucchini halves on a cookie sheet and spoon meat mixture into zucchinis. Cover with shredded cheese, and black pepper and Italian seasoning.
5. Bake 15–18 minutes.

(without cheese)

ITALIAN STUFFED BELL PEPPERS

If you want a healthy alternative to rice in this recipe, try quinoa. Not only is it a superfood and full of protein and other nutrients you need, but it is very flavorful in this Italian dish. Yummy with a salad!—Chelsea

Makes 8 bell pepper halves | Time: 1 hour

1½ cups uncooked quinoa or 1 cup uncooked rice
2 tsp. chicken bouillon (or enough bouillon for 2 cups worth
    of broth)
2 boneless, skinless chicken breasts
1 Tbsp. oil
½ cup diced sweet onion
1 cup frozen mixed veggies, thawed
1 (24-oz.) jar spaghetti sauce
4 red, yellow, orange, or green bell peppers
2 cups shredded cheese
1 Tbsp. Italian seasoning

1. Preheat oven to 375 degrees.
2. Follow cooking directions on quinoa or rice bag and add chicken bouillon to the water.
3. Dice the chicken and place in a pan with oil. Stir on high for about 5 minutes, then add onions and mixed veggies. Cook on medium for another 2–3 minutes.
4. Add cooked quinoa and spaghetti sauce to pan and mix.
5. Spray or oil a cookie sheet or 9 x 13 pan. Remove seeds from peppers and then cut in half vertically. Spoon stuffing into each bell pepper half (about ¾ cup) and then cover with cheese.

6. Bake 30 minutes. Allow to cool for about 5 minutes and then eat away!

(without cheese)

ITALIAN ENCHILADAS

This is a delicious alternative to traditional enchiladas.—Chelsea

Makes 14 enchiladas | Time: 45 minutes

3–4 boneless, skinless chicken breasts, diced
1 Tbsp. oil
1 small zucchini, diced
½ red bell pepper, diced
½ red onion, diced
2 (15-oz.) jars alfredo sauce, divided
1 Tbsp. pesto
2½ cups shredded cheese, divided
2 Tbsp. Italian seasoning
¼ cup sun dried tomatoes, optional.
14 corn tortillas

1. Preheat oven to 350 degrees.
2. Cook chicken in oil on medium-high heat for about 8 minutes then shred with a fork.
3. Add chicken, zucchini, red bell pepper, onion, ½ cup alfredo sauce, pesto, ½ cup shredded cheese, Italian seasoning, and the optional sun-dried tomatoes to a bowl and mix.
4. Wrap tortillas in slightly damp cloth and heat in the microwave for about a minute or until pliable. Fill center of each tortilla with meat mixture, roll, and then place in a 9 x 13 dish in rows, seam-side down.

5. Add 1½ full jars alfredo sauce evenly over tortillas. Sprinkle with remaining cheese.

6. Bake in the oven for 30 minutes.

(depending on alfredo sauce)

SMOTHERED CHICKEN ENCHILADAS

Creamy and filling, these enchiladas are just divine and make a great meal to feed friends and roommates. Don't want to share? They also make great leftovers.—Ashley

Makes 4 enchiladas | Time: 30 minutes

½ Tbsp. vegetable oil
½ lb. chicken breast, diced
½ medium onion, chopped
4 (8-inch) flour tortillas
¾ cup grated Monterey Jack cheese or Mexican blend cheese, divided
2 Tbsp. butter
2 Tbsp. flour
1 cup chicken broth
½ cup sour cream
1 (4-oz.) can chopped green chilies

GLUTEN-FREE TIP: Use softened corn tortillas and 1 tablespoon cornstarch in place of the flour for the roux.

1. Heat oil in frying pan over medium-high heat. Add chicken and onion and cook until chicken is done through.

2. Divide chicken and onion between tortillas. Divide ½ cup cheese between tortillas.

3. Lightly grease a 9 x 13 dish. Roll enchiladas and place seam-side down in the dish.

4. Melt butter in a medium saucepan and stir in flour to make a roux. Gradually whisk in chicken broth and bring to a boil, stirring frequently. Remove from heat and stir in sour cream and green chiles. Pour sauce evenly over enchiladas.

6. Top with remaining cheese and bake at 400 degrees for 20 minutes. When the enchiladas are ready, the cheese will be melted and the sauce at the edges of the dish will be bubbly.

(with corn)

SWEET POTATO ENCHILADAS

Enjoy these healthier enchiladas on a bed of lettuce or rice and top with fresh tomatoes and avocado slices.—Chelsea

Makes 6–7 servings | Time: 1 hour

1 medium sweet potato, thinly sliced
2 boneless, skinless chicken breasts, diced
1 Tbsp. oil
2 cups corn
½ cup chopped green bell pepper
3 tsp. minced cilantro
2 garlic cloves, minced
2 cups shredded cheese, divided
½ tsp. cumin powder
1 tsp. chili powder
1 cup crema (Mexican table cream or sour cream), divided
2 cups salsa verde
14 corn tortillas

1. Preheat oven to 350 degrees.
2. Boil diced sweet potatoes in a large pot of water for 10 minutes or until potatoes are tender.
3. Cook chicken in oil on medium heat for about 8 minutes or until no longer pink. Allow to cool and then shred with a fork.
4. Add corn, green bell pepper, cilantro, garlic, ½ cup shredded cheese, cumin, chili powder, cooked sweet potatoes, and shredded chicken in a large bowl and mix.
5. Spread ½ cup crema on the bottom of a 9 x 13 pan.
6. Wrap 14 tortillas in a damp cloth and microwave for about 1 minute or until pliable.

7. Place two to three spoonfuls of sweet potato mixture in the middle of each corn tortilla, roll it, and place tortilla, seam-side down, in the pan.

8. Mix salsa verde and ½ cup crema in a bowl and spread over enchiladas. Bake for 20 minutes. Then cover with remaining cheese and bake for another 8–10 minutes.

MONGOLIAN BEEF

Served hot over fragrant jasmine rice, this beef straight out of nice Chinese restaurants will taste like you spent hours cooking it.—Ashley

Makes 3 servings | Time: 30 minutes

2 tsp. extra-virgin olive oil
½ tsp. minced ginger
1 Tbsp. minced garlic
½ cup soy sauce
½ cup water
¾ cup brown sugar
1 lb. flank steak
¼ cup cornstarch
2 green onions
2 cups jasmine rice
olive oil for frying, about ½ cup

1. In a medium saucepan over medium heat, heat 2 teaspoons oil, watching that it doesn't get too hot or it will splatter with some of the other ingredients. Add ginger and garlic to the pan. Quickly add both soy sauce and water before the ginger scorches.

2. Dissolve brown sugar in the sauce. Raise the heat and boil for about 2 minutes until thickened. Remove from heat and set aside to cool.

3. Using a very sharp knife, slice flank steak thinly, cutting against the grain. Toss slices in cornstarch to apply a very thin coating. Set the meat aside for a few minutes, allowing the coating to stick.

4. While waiting, slice the green onions into ½-inch lengths.

5. In a different saucepan with a lid, bring 4 cups water to a boil, and add jasmine rice. Remove from heat and cover, stirring occasionally to keep from sticking to the sides of the pan. Fluff with a fork when done, about 20–25 minutes.

6. Heat the remaining oil in a wok or deep skillet. Add the beef to the oil and sauté until the beef has just darkened on the edges, stirring around for an even cooking.

7. Use a slotted spoon to scoop out the meat, and set aside on a plate. Pour out the oil into a non-styrofoam paper cup. Add the meat back to the wok, and simmer for 1 minute. Add the sauce and cook for 1 minute, adding onions when done. Cook for 1 more minute, and then remove the beef and onions with a slotted spoon. Use the excess sauce to store the meat for leftovers so that it stays flavorful and moist. Serve over rice.

ASIAN CHICKEN LETTUCE BOATS

This Asian chicken and rice nestled inside a lettuce leaf is a fun and easy dish to make. Perfect for lots of leftovers or to feed your roommates. It's delicious and healthy!—Chelsea

Makes about 15–18 lettuce boats
Time: 30 minutes, depending on rice

2 cups cooked white or brown rice
2 lb. ground chicken (or turkey)
2 cloves garlic, minced
1 red bell pepper, finely chopped
½ cup finely chopped yellow onion
½ cup finely chopped zucchini
½ cup hoisin sauce (Asian section of the grocery store)
2 Tbsp. soy sauce
½ tsp. salt
½ tsp. black pepper

3 green onions, thinly sliced rounds
1 Tbsp. rice vinegar
2 romaine lettuce hearts
sriracha to drizzle

> **COOKING TIP:**
> Brown rice needs to be soaked for several hours before cooking it.

1. Start rice immediately by following instructions on the bag. About 1 cup of uncooked rice yields 2 cups of cooked rice.

2. Brown chicken in a pan and soak up grease with a paper towel.

3. Add garlic, red bell pepper, onion, and zucchini to pan on medium-high heat.

4. Mix hoisin sauce, soy sauce, salt, and pepper in a

small bowl and then pour into pan and mix well.

5. When rice is done, add rice, green onions, and rice vinegar to the pan. Cook for another five minutes, stirring often.

6. Rinse romaine lettuce hearts and break off long pieces. Fill the center of each "boat" with meat mixture and lightly drizzle sriracha on top.

(with gluten-free
soy sauce)

CHINESE FRIED EGG SPAGHETTI

Here is a little taste of a traditional Asian dish you may not have discovered yet. It's easy and savory! The time this recipe takes is completely dependent upon how long your rice takes to cook.—Chelsea

Makes 5 servings | Time: 30 Minutes

2 cups rice, cooked
1 lb. ground hamburger
3 cups frozen mixed veggies
1 (24-oz.) jar spaghetti sauce
5 eggs
1 Tbsp. oil

1. Brown hamburger in a pan. Remove grease with a paper towel and then add frozen veggies. Stir until warm and well thawed out.

2. Pour spaghetti sauce in pan and mix together. Turn heat to low and place lid over sauce.

3. When rice is almost done, add oil to another pan and turn the heat to high. Allow pan to warm then crack an egg in pan. For a runny yolk, allow the egg to cook on high for about 90 seconds then flip and allow an additional 30 seconds. For a well-cooked egg, cook each side for about 2 minutes. Make 1 egg per bowl.

4. Place desired amount of rice in a bowl with a

generous amount of meat sauce. Top with a fried egg and eat away!

PINEAPPLE CURRY

Impress all your friends! Curry like this tastes more complicated than it really is. I learned recently that you can make this in a slow cooker. Just add all ingredients but bell peppers and pineapple and set on Low for a couple of hours. Add peppers and pineapple before serving and pour over rice.—Ashley

Makes 4–6 servings | Time: 25 minutes

2 cups uncooked jasmine rice
1 quart water
2 skinless, boneless chicken breast halves, cubed
¼ cup red curry paste
2 (13.5-oz.) cans coconut milk, divided
3 Tbsp. fish sauce
¼ cup sugar
1½ cups sliced bamboo shoots, drained
1 red bell pepper, julienned
½ small onion, chopped
1 cup drained pineapple chunks
sweet chili paste, optional

COOKING TIP:
If you prefer spicier curry, don't add extra curry paste. Many store-bought bottles are too expensive to spend on one batch of curry. Instead, add just a bit of sweet chili paste.

1. Bring rice and water to a boil in a pot. Reduce heat to low, cover, and simmer 25 minutes.

2. In a wok or large skillet, cook the cubed chicken until done through. Meanwhile, in a separate bowl, mix curry paste and 1 can coconut milk. Transfer to the wok or skillet. Add in remaining can of coconut milk, fish

sauce, sugar, and bamboo shoots. Bring to a boil.

3. Mix the red bell pepper and onion into the wok. Continue cooking 10 minutes, until peppers are tender. Remove from heat, and stir in pineapple. Serve over cooked rice in bowls.

THAI CHICKEN TACOS

We have all heard of normal Mexican tacos, but what about Thai chicken tacos? Yes, they exist! Enjoy the subtle flavoring of veggies mixed with chicken, topped off with a delicious peanut sauce.—Chelsea

Makes 3–4 servings
Time: 30 minutes (marinate for at least two hours)

Chicken and marinade

2 large boneless, skinless chicken breasts
¼ cup lime juice
¼ cup soy sauce
3 Tbsp. brown sugar
3 Tbsp. olive oil (or vegetable), divided
1 Tbsp. fish sauce
1 Tbsp. sriracha
2 cloves garlic, minced
2 tsp. peeled and minced ginger
⅓ cup chopped green onions

> **TIME-SAVING TIP:**
> Check grocery store for a tube of already peeled and smashed ginger.

Toppings

10–12 corn tortillas
1½ cup purple cabbage, chopped
½ cup shredded carrots
½ red bell pepper, diced
¼ cup chopped green onions

Peanut Sauce

2 Tbsp. hot water
⅓ cup creamy peanut butter
2½ Tbsp. brown sugar
1 Tbsp. lime juice
1 Tbsp. soy sauce
1 tsp. peeled and finely minced ginger
1 tsp. sriracha

1. Dice chicken and place in a plastic Ziplock bag. Add lime juice, soy sauce, brown sugar, 2 tablespoons oil, fish sauce, sriracha, garlic, ginger, and green onions into bag. Squeeze bag to combine ingredients. Allow chicken to marinate for at least 2 hours.

2. Add 1 tablespoon oil to a frying pan with chicken. Only add ¼ cup marinade to frying pan. Cook chicken on medium high for 8–10 minutes or until cooked.

3. Combine all ingredients for the peanut sauce in a bowl and mix well.

4. Wrap tortillas in a slightly damp cloth and warm in the microwave.

5. Add chicken, purple cabbage, shredded carrots, red bell peppers, and green onions to a tortilla. Then drizzle peanut sauce over top.

(use gluten-free soy sauce)

TACOS

Simple meals like tacos are a must-have for busy college students. Save some cash by keeping homemade taco seasoning in an airtight, resealable bag.—Ashley

Makes 8 servings | Time: 25 minutes

Homemade Taco Seasoning
½ Tbsp. chili powder
¼ tsp. garlic powder
¼ tsp. onion powder
¼ tsp. dried oregano
½ tsp. paprika
1½ tsp cumin
1 tsp. salt
1 tsp. pepper

1 lb. ground beef
hard or soft taco shells

Toppings
red peppers, julienned
shredded Mexican cheese blend
lettuce
salsa
sour cream
pico de gallo

1. In a small bowl, combine seasoning ingredients.
2. Brown beef in a large skillet over medium-high heat until completely done. Using a slotted spoon, remove the meat and set aside in a large bowl. Drain away the excess fat. Return beef to skillet.

3. Pour in ½ cup water and seasoning and stir well. Simmer until the liquid has absorbed into the beef, and remove from heat.

4. Fill tortillas or shells with meat and your favorite taco toppings.

(without cheese or
sour cream)

TACO-ZAGNA

My friend Sarah Durtschi perfected this recipe, which lasts for plenty of meals and is a fun, easy Mexican twist on lasagna.—Ashley

Makes 10–15 servings | Time: 45 minutes

2 Tbsp. butter

1 box Mexican style Rice-A-Roni

1 bag tater tots

2 cans Nalley Original chili con carne with beans

2 lb. lean ground beef

2 packets Old El Paso Original taco seasoning mix

2 family-sized packages of small soft shell tortillas

2 packages presliced medium cheddar cheese (shredded cheese works as well.)

1 medium-sized bottle of Pace mild picante salsa

1. Preheat oven to 425 degrees.

2. Melt butter in a skillet over medium heat. Add rice to brown. Add 2¼ cups water and bring to a boil. Then add seasoning packet that comes with rice. Turn heat to low, cover, and simmer for about 20 minutes.

3. Place tater tots on a cookie sheet and bake 20–24 minutes. Meanwhile, warm chili.

4. In a separate skillet, brown ground beef. Add in 1⅓ cups water and stir in taco seasoning. Bring to a boil, and then lower heat to allow sauce to thicken.

5. In a 9 x 13 pan, layer as follows: soft taco shells,

chili, sliced cheese, rice, soft taco shells, browned beef, salsa, cheese, tater tots, cheese. Serve and enjoy!

(depending on tater tots)

FAJITAS

The steak does take a while to marinate here, but it's easy enough to put together before you go to class or work. Then you can come back to extremely flavorful and juicy steak for easy, tender steak fajitas.—Ashley

Makes 8 fajitas | Time: 2 hours 15 minutes

Meat and marinade
½ cup olive oil
⅓ cup soy sauce
¼ cup vinegar
2 Tbsp. lemon juice
1½ Tbsp. Worcestershire sauce
1 Tbsp. mustard (Dijon is the best)
2 cloves garlic, minced
½ tsp. pepper
1½ lb. flank steak

8 tortillas

Toppings
red peppers, julienned
shredded Mexican cheese blend
lettuce
salsa
sour cream
pico de gallo

1. Combine all marinade ingredients but the steak in a gallon-sized resealable bag. Shake well. Add the steak and shake again to coat thoroughly. Seal and refrigerate for as long as possible, at least 2 hours, but 6 if you can spare it.

2. Preheat a skillet or grill to medium-high heat, and brush with oil. Place steaks on the grill and discard marinade. Grill until done to preference.

3. Using a very sharp knife, slice the steak against the grain into thin strips. Fill flour tortillas with the meat and your favorite fajita toppings. Serve warm.

(with corn tortillas)

FAJITA PASTA

With a host of fresh flavors and a little creamy spice, this pasta dish is bound to be a favorite. If you want something less spicy, try Rotel tomatoes without green chilies.—Chelsea

Makes 5 servings | Time: 30 minutes

2 large boneless, skinless chicken breasts, diced
2 Tbsp. oil, divided
1 (1-oz.) packet (or 3 Tbsp.) taco seasoning
1 medium-sized red onion, chopped
1½ green bell peppers, chopped
2 cloves garlic, minced
2 cups water (1 extra cup for gluten-free noodles)
2 tsp. chicken bouillon (Better Than Bouillon brand)
½ cup crema (Mexican table cream, heavy cream, or evaporated milk)
1 (10-oz.) can Rotel tomatoes with green chilies
1 (12-oz.) package penne noodles

1. Cook chicken in 1 tablespoon oil in a large pan for about 7–8 minutes on medium-high heat. Drain extra water and stir in taco seasoning packet. Set chicken aside in a medium-sized bowl.

2. Cook red onion, green bell pepper, and garlic in 1 tablespoon oil in same pan until slightly blackened. Add veggies to the bowl with the chicken.

3. In the same pan, add water, bouillon, crema, Rotel tomatoes, and noodles. Stir contents and bring to a bowl. Cover and simmer on medium-low heat for 15 minutes or until liquid is well absorbed and noodles are cooked. If you have too much leftover liquid, continue to cook for an additional 3–5 minutes.

4. Add veggies and chicken to pot and cook for 3 more minutes, stirring occasionally.

(with gluten-free noodles)

BURRITO BOWL

Tired of scrubbing tons of dishes after making dinner? This recipe is contained in one bowl of heaven. Full of chicken, cheese, and the perfect accent of spice, it is delicious to eat with tortillas or tortilla chips.—Chelsea

Makes 5–6 servings
Time: 35–45 minutes (depending on type of rice)

2 boneless, skinless chicken breasts, diced
1 Tbsp. avocado oil

½ cup diced sweet onion
½ cup diced red bell pepper
½ cup sliced black olives
⅓ cup chunky salsa
1 (14-oz.) can Mexican stewed tomatoes, squished
1 (10-oz.) can Rotel tomatoes with green chilies
1 (15.25-oz.) can black beans, drained and rinsed
1 (15.25-oz.) can corn, drained
3 Tbsp. or 1 packet taco seasoning
1 cup uncooked rice
2 tsp. chicken bouillon (Better Than Bouillon brand)
2 cups water

Optional Toppings
cheese
sour cream
avocado, diced
green onions, thinly sliced

1. Cook chicken in oil on medium-high heat for 7–8 minutes in a pot. Drain extra liquid then add everything else (apart from toppings) and stir.

2. Bring to a light boil and then cover pan and reduce heat to low for 15–30 minutes, depending on your rice. Stir rice every 8 minutes. Taste rice to make sure it is soft and well cooked.

3. Add desired toppings!

(check taco seasoning packet)   (without cheese and
                                          sour cream)

CARNE ASADA TORTA (MEXICAN SANDWICH)

This is one of my favorite Mexican lunches! Traditionally people use tolera bread, which can be found in a Hispanic market or grocery store. You can also use normal bread or tortillas. I recommend marinating the meat overnight!—Chelsea

Makes about 4 sandwiches or 10 corn tortillas
Time: 20 minutes to cook (marinate for at least two hours)

Marinade

2 tsp. garlic powder
2 tsp. onion powder
2 tsp. smoked paprika
1½ tsp. cumin
1½ tsp. chili powder
1 tsp. salt
½ tsp. black pepper
½ tsp. ground ginger
1 garlic clove, minced
2 Tbsp. lime juice
4 Tbsp. oil, divided
1 lb. thinly-sliced steak (stir fry steak works great)

COOKING TIP:
Some grocery stores have ginger in a tube, which saves time. Otherwise, ginger needs to be peeled and smashed.

Sandwich

4–5 large rolls
½ (16-oz.) can refried beans
1 avocado, smashed
1 cup cheese

Optional Toppings

Lettuce
Tomato, sliced
Salsa
Crema or sour cream

1. Mix marinade ingredients together, reserving 1 tablespoon oil, and place in a large plastic bag with steak. Shake bag to make sure marinade spreads all over meat.

2. Place bag in the fridge for 2–12 hours. The longer it marinates, the more delicious it will be.

3. Heat remaining tablespoon oil in a pan on medium-high heat. Cook meat for about 10 minutes or until no longer pink.

4. Heat up refried beans on the stove.

5. Warm up rolls in the microwave and then cut in half. Spread refried beans and sprinkle cheese on one half and avocado on the other. Add meat, lettuce, tomato, salsa, and sour cream/crema to sandwich.

Only make the amount of sandwiches you need at one time.

(with corn tortillas or gluten-free bread)   (without cheese or crema/ sour cream)

DINNER SIDES

CAPRESE TOMATOES

These are great party sides that look like you spent forever on them!
They take a caprese salad and make it into finger food.—Ashley

Makes 6 servings | Time: 15 minutes

6 tomatoes
1 cup feta cheese
5–6 large basil leaves, chopped
1 Tbsp. olive oil
salt
pepper

1. Preheat oven to 400 degrees.
2. Slice the top of the tomato about ½ inch below the stem. Using a spoon, scoop out the inside of the tomato, being careful not to pierce the skin.
3. Mix feta and basil. Spoon the mixture into each of the tomatoes. Season tomato caps with salt and pepper, and drizzle with olive oil. Put caps back on tomatoes.
4. Lightly grease a baking dish and fill with the tomatoes, spacing them evenly. Bake for about 10 minutes or until tomatoes have softened and look wrinkled.

STRAWBERRY BASIL KEBABS

These have a unique tang to them, and they're very simple to make. Serve these at barbecues or outdoor gatherings, or just make one for yourself!—Ashley

Makes about 3 skewers | Time: 5 minutes

5 strawberries
10 large basil leaves
balsamic vinegar OR Balsamic Vinegar Reduction (page 79)
3 bamboo skewers, soaked*

1. Slice strawberries in half after trimming the top. Wash basil leaves thoroughly, and thread onto skewers, alternating with berries. Brush balsamic vinegar over the skewers.

2. Heat grill to medium. Place skewers so that the cut sides of the strawberries are down and grill for about 30 seconds, or until the berries sizzle. Quickly brush again with balsamic vinegar, and remove from grill. Serve warm.

Soaking the skewers keeps them from scorching in the oven while you're grilling.

ITALIAN GARLIC POTATOES

Don't even worry about adding ketchup to these. They are tasty enough all alone.—Chelsea

Makes 2–3 servings | Time: 20 minutes

3–4 medium potatoes, thinly sliced
1½ Tbsp. oil, divided
½ tsp. salt
1 tsp. Italian seasoning
½ tsp. garlic powder
¼ cup parmesan cheese
1 pinch black pepper
add a light handful of shredded cheese (cheddar or mozzarella), optional

1. Add potatoes slices and ½ tablespoon oil to a pan on high heat. Cover pan for 10 minutes and stir often to prevent burning.

2. Uncover pan and add salt, Italian seasoning, garlic powder, parmesan cheese, and black pepper to potatoes and mix together. Stir for another 5 minutes or until potatoes are soft and a few are golden brown.

ITALIAN NOODLE SALAD

Enjoy this zesty noodle salad as a light main course or a perfect side. Makes plenty for your roommates!—Chelsea

Makes 6–7 servings | Time: 20–25 minutes

1 (16-oz.) package macaroni noodles
1 cup chopped red onion
¼ cup parmesan cheese
½ cup diced olives
1 orange bell pepper, chopped
1 cup chopped small zucchini
¼–½ cup Italian dressing

1. Cook noodles according to package until soft then strain and run them under cold water.

2. In a medium-sized bowl add all ingredients and stir. Add more Italian dressing based on preference of the zesty flavor. If you eat this salad as leftovers, you will probably need to add more dressing. Gluten-free noodles also soak up a LOT of dressing and are best eaten within the first two days.

(gluten-free
noodles)

CHILI GARLIC DEVILED EGGS

These might look fancy but they are super easy to make! Now you can finally contribute something to your Thanksgiving dinner!—Chelsea

Makes 4–6 servings | Time: 30 minutes

6 eggs
3 Tbsp. mayonnaise
1 Tbsp. chili garlic sauce (Asian section of grocery store)
½ Tbsp. lime juice
¼ tsp. salt
finely chopped cilantro to garnish

1. Place 6 eggs in a pot and add enough cold water to cover the eggs by 1 inch. Bring water to a boil on medium heat. Once water is at a rolling boil, cover with a lid and remove from heat. Let eggs sit for 12 minutes.
2. Run eggs under cold water for 2 minutes. Also run cold water over each egg while you peel away the shell.
3. Cut eggs in half (vertically). Scoop out egg yolk and place in another bowl.
4. Add mayonnaise, chili garlic sauce, salt, and lime juice to the egg yolks. Use a fork to combine ingredients.
5. Transfer your mashed yolk mixture into a Ziplock bag. Seal bag then cut off one of the bottom corners. Squeeze the yolk mixture back into the egg white holes. Garnish with chopped cilantro and chill in the refrigerator.

SWEET POTATO CHIPS

Whether you eat these during your Thanksgiving feast or as chips, the sweet taste makes you forget that these are HEALTHY for you. Sweet potatoes are more in season during the months of October through December. This side is a great addition to the Paprika Brown Sugar Chicken (page 100), Caramelized Ham and Cheese Rolls (page 126), and Salt and Pepper Pork (page 103).—Chelsea

Makes 2 servings | Time: 25–30 minutes

1 large sweet potato
1½ Tbsp. oil (I recommend coconut oil)
salt and pepper to taste

> **HEALTH TIP:**
> Sweet potatoes are a high source of fiber and contain almost no fat.

1. Preheat oven to 375 degrees.
2. Slice sweet potato in ⅛-inch slices. Place on a cookie sheet side by side and bake for 30 minutes or until soft.
3. Place in a bowl and mix in oil and salt and pepper.

SPEEDY BBQ BAKED BEANS

Don't miss out on these creamy BBQ Baked Beans! They take seconds to make and will be a huge hit for summer BBQ parties! If you want to make this dish for a party though, I recommend at least doubling it. Make these beans with the Buffalo Chicken Roll (page 128 or Mom's Cups (page 104).—Chelsea

Makes 2–3 servings | Time: 10 minutes

1 (28-oz.) can Bush's Original Baked Beans
¼ cup Mexican stewed tomatoes
½ cup instant mashed potato mix

1. Place beans in a pot on medium heat. Squish stewed tomatoes with your hands and add to beans.

2. Once beans are hot, add instant mashed potato and stir frequently until beans thicken.

PARMESAN RICE BALLS (ARANCINI)

Gooey and cheesy, these are a great way to use leftover rice. You can also make it from scratch using arborio (risotto) rice to get it at its stickiest.—Ashley

Makes about 15 rice balls | Time: 50 minutes

1 package arborio rice OR 3–4 cups leftover moist or sticky rice
¼ cup shredded parmesan
¼ cup shredded mozzarella
1 egg
1 tsp. water
1½ cups panko or bread crumbs
marinara sauce

COOKING TIP:
If your rice doesn't stick together well enough to form a ball, heat in the microwave for 1–2 minutes. It should then be sticky enough to hold its shape.

1. If you are using a package of arborio rice, prepare according to directions, and let cool completely for at least 30 minutes in the fridge. Combine the cheeses in a small bowl and set aside.

2. Preheat oven to 400 degrees. Take small handfuls of rice. In the palm of your hand, form a patty with a small dip in the center. Fill with cheese blend, and roll the rice into a ball around it.

3. In a small dish, mix egg and water. Dip the rice balls into the egg, and let the excess drip off. Roll in the panko or bread crumbs until fully coated.

4. Place the coated rice balls on a baking sheet, and bake for about 15 minutes. Serve warm with marinara sauce.

These can also be fried. Heat oil to 375 degrees and fry 4–5 at a time until golden brown.

Variation: Southwest Rice Ball

1 package taco seasoning
4 Tbsp. green chiles
½ cup pepper jack cheese
1 Tbsp. ranch seasoning
1 cup sour cream
1 avocado, peeled and seeded
1 Tbsp. lemon juice

1. Mix the taco seasoning and chiles into the cooked rice. Following the directions above, replace cheeses with pepper jack. Bake for 15 minutes at 400 degrees and serve warm.

2. To make the sauce, combine ranch seasoning, sour cream, avocado, and lemon juice.

PILAFI (GREEK LEMON RICE)

Serve this savory, lemony rice with Greek or Italian recipes. It goes especially well with Souvlaki (page 48), Gyros (page 50), Rosemary Lemon Chicken (page 101), and Piadinas (page 44)!

Makes 2–3 servings | Time: 25 minutes

1 cup chicken broth

½ cup water

¾ cup uncooked basmati or jasmine rice

1 medium onion, diced

1 Tbsp. oil

½ tsp. dried dill

½ tsp. dried mint

2 Tbsp. lemon juice

½ cup crumbled feta (optional)

1. Bring broth, water, and rice to a boil. Reduce the heat to low, cover, and allow to cook until soft, about 20 minutes.

2. While it cooks, sauté onion over medium heat in oil until soft, about 5 minutes. In a small dish, stir together spices and lemon juice.

3. When the rice is done, add the onion mixture and lemon juice mixture, stirring and fluffing the cooked rice with a fork to combine. Cover and keep warm for about 5–10 minutes. Serve with feta sprinkled on top.

If you have a rice cooker, combine rice, broth, and water in a rice cooker and turn it to Cook. Follow the rest of the recipe accordingly. After adding the lemon mixture and the onion mixture, close the cover on the rice cooker and set to Keep Warm for 5–10 minutes.

SPANISH RICE

Better than regular rice, this savory and simple side goes well with Mexican meals and can be used to top off a taco.—Ashley

Makes 1–2 servings | Time: 20 minutes

1½ cups uncooked rice
2 cups chicken broth
1 cup salsa

Over medium-low heat, add all ingredients to a large pot with a lid or to a rice cooker. Cover and simmer about 20 minutes or until all liquid has been absorbed, keeping an eye on the rice so it doesn't burn and stick to the sides. Fluff with a fork and serve.

BREAD

AND OTHER

DELICIOUS BAKED GOODS

CLOUD BREAD

This is ridiculously easy to make, and as a bonus, it's gluten-free. You can use this in place of the bread for Bruschetta (page 72), in place of hamburger buns, or just as a snack.—Ashley

Makes 10–12 buns, depending on size | Time: 25 minutes

3 eggs
3 Tbsp. cream cheese
¼ tsp. baking powder

1. Preheat oven to 300 degrees and grease a baking sheet. Using a series of small bowls, separate the yolks from the whites. Do not let any yolk get into the white.

2. Mix the yolks and the cream cheese together until smooth.

3. In a separate bowl, beat the whites and baking powder together until mixture forms fluffy, firm peaks. Carefully fold this mixture into the yolk mixture, being careful not to damage the fluffiness of the white mixture.

4. Acting as quickly as possible to keep the mixture from dissolving, spoon onto the baking sheet. Bake for 17–20 minutes, and then broil for 1 minute or until the bread is golden brown. Remove from oven and let cool.

Variations: Mix 1 tablespoon honey with egg yolk mixture for a sweeter bread.

Sprinkle rosemary or other herbs over the bread before baking.

EASY BRAZILIAN CHEESE BREAD

Whenever I'm able to afford Brazilian grills, one of my favorite sides is pão de queijo, or cheese bread. Once you learn how simple this is to make, it's truly addicting!

The best cheese to use here is probably queso fresco, a soft Mexican cheese I find at Walmart. However, feta or goat cheese also work well.—Ashley

Makes 24 rolls | Time: 25 minutes

1½ cups tapioca flour
1 egg
½ cup grated or crumbled cheese of your choice
⅔ cup milk
⅓ cup olive oil
1 tsp. salt

1. Preheat oven to 400 degrees. Lightly grease a mini muffin tin and set aside.

2. In a food processor or blender, blend all ingredients until smooth. Pour mixture into each muffin tin cup, leaving a little bit of room at the top of each one.

3. Bake for 15–20 minutes until the rolls have risen into puffy shapes and are golden brown. Remove from rack and let cool slightly. Serve warm.

ZUCCHINI BREADSTICKS

These breadsticks are a super yummy, healthy alternative to traditional breadsticks. The bread is a mix of flour and shredded zucchini, so much of the guilt for eating one too many can fly out the window. Sprinkle with cheese and dip in hot marinara sauce.—Chelsea

Makes about 8 long pieces | Time: 40 minutes

3 cups grated zucchini (about 2 medium-sized zucchini)
1 cup flour
2 eggs
½ cup mozzarella cheese
1 tsp. salt
1 tsp. Italian seasoning
1½–2 cups shredded cheddar cheese
marinara sauce for dipping

1. Preheat oven to 450 degrees.
2. Squish grated zucchini in a thin rag to remove excess liquid.
3. Mix zucchini, flour, eggs, mozzarella cheese, salt, and Italian seasoning in a bowl.
4. Oil a 9 x 13 pan, wet hands, then evenly spread dough throughout base of pan. Bake for 20 minutes. Some college apartments or homes have unpredictable ovens. Check dough to make sure it has finished cooking. It should be easy to lift out of the pan.
5. Cover with cheddar cheese and an additional sprinkle of Italian seasoning. Bake for another 2 minutes, or until cheese is melted.
6. Warm up marinara sauce in the microwave (be sure to cover it with a paper towel) and then dip away!

(with gluten-free flour)

GLUTEN-FREE BREAD FOR MOM'S CUPS

Gluten-free bread can be pretty temperamental, but this recipe works great for several of the recipes in this book that use dough. If you are unfamiliar with gluten-free bread, just know that it lacks the binding agent that helps it stick to itself, so the texture may be a bit different. It also requires more water than a normal bread recipe. This recipe will work with normal flour, but you might need to add a little extra flour.—Chelsea

Time: 10–15 minutes to make, about 20–30 minutes to bake depending on the recipe you use with this bread

2 Tbsp. brown sugar (for more salty meals, only add 1 Tbsp. of brown sugar)
1 Tbsp. yeast
¼ cup warm water
1½ cups milk
2 Tbsp. honey
2 Tbsp. oil
1 Tbsp. cider vinegar
3 eggs, room temperature
3¾ cups Namaste perfect flour blend or another gluten-free flour option (I have found Namaste to be my favorite gluten-free flour. I found it at Costco)
½ cup cornstarch
1 tsp. salt

1. Mix brown sugar and yeast in warm (120 degrees) water. Warm milk in a separate bowl and add honey, oil, and cider vinegar. Beat eggs and pour into milk mix. After allowing yeast mixture to sit for at least 5 minutes or until it begins to rise, mix with milk mixture.

2. Add flour, cornstarch, and salt to a medium-sized bowl. Pour liquid mixture in with dry ingredients. Knead dough for three minutes or until completely mixed. Now it is ready!

CHEESE PULL-APART BREAD

Gooey mozzarella and garlic butter make this party food utterly irresistible! It's easy to make with almost any soft, easily melted cheese and a loaf of crusty bread for parties or get-togethers.—Ashley

Makes 1 loaf | Time: 20 minutes

½ cup butter, softened
1½ tsp. minced garlic
¾ tsp. salt
1 crusty loaf bread, such as sourdough or artisan bread
1 cup shredded mozzarella cheese

1. Preheat oven to 375 degrees. In a small bowl, combine butter, garlic, and salt. Melt in microwave in 10-second bursts.

2. Using a sharp knife, slice bread diagonally on both sides to form diamond shapes in the crust. Do not cut all the way through the bread. Open up slices and drizzle butter inside. Stuff shredded mozzarella cheese into the slices as well until all are filled with both butter and cheese.

3. Wrap loaf in foil and bake for 15 minutes until the cheese has completely melted. Serve immediately.

(EASY)

JUST DESSERTS

CHOCOLATE PEANUT BUTTER BANANA BREAD

This banana bread is so good you can eat it with ice cream.—Chelsea

Makes about 18 squares | Time: 40 minutes

3 large ripe frozen bananas, thawed
⅓ cup butter, melted
¾ cup brown sugar
1 tsp. salt (½ tsp. if using salted butter)
1 large egg, beaten
1 tsp. vanilla extract
1¼ cups flour
¼ cup coco powder
¼ tsp. ground allspice
1 tsp. baking soda
½ cup peanut butter and chocolate chip morsels

1. Preheat oven to 350 degrees.
2. Use a blender to purée the bananas or smash them with a fork until smooth. Stir in the melted butter, brown sugar, salt, beaten egg, and vanilla extract.
3. In another bowl, mix the flour, cocoa powder, ground allspice, and baking soda together. Add to wet ingredients until just barely mixed. Fold in peanut butter and chocolate chip morsels.
4. Pour batter into an oiled 9 x 13 dish. Bake for 25–30 minutes. If a knife inserted into the center of the pan comes up clean, your banana bread is done!

(with gluten-free flour)

FLOURLESS PEANUT BUTTER BANANA MUFFINS

Craving peanut butter banana goodness but not patient enough to make banana bread? Here is your answer!—Chelsea

Makes 12 muffins | Time: 15–20 minutes

1 ripe banana
1 egg
½ cup peanut butter, heaping
3 Tbsp. brown sugar
1 tsp. vanilla extract
¼ tsp. baking soda
½ cup semi-sweet chocolate chips

1. Preheat oven to 400 degrees.
2. Mix all ingredients together in a blender until creamy or smash and mix with a fork.
3. Oil muffin tin or use muffin cups (we recommend this! It makes a HUGE difference with cleanup) then distribute batter evenly between each cup.
4. Bake for 10–12 minutes. Tops should be springy to the touch.

(without chocolate)

CHERRY CHOCOLATE CAKE

This is my grandma's famous cake, popular among our family and friends. Best of all, it can be made from a boxed cake mix with a couple extra ingredients to make it super moist.—Ashley

Makes 12–15 servings | Time: 45 minutes

1 dark chocolate cake mix (e.g. Devil's Food Cake)
1 (4-oz.) pkg. dry chocolate pudding
1 cup sour cream
1 (21-oz.) can cherry pie filling
chocolate frosting
fresh or maraschino cherries, optional

1. Preheat oven to 350 degrees, and lightly grease a cake pan. Prepare cake mix according to directions on the box, adding pudding and sour cream to the mixture. Blend well.

2. Pour in cherry pie filling, and fold into the chocolate mix. Spread cake mix into the pan and bake cake for 35–40 minutes, or until a toothpick inserted into the center comes out clean. Let cool completely.

3. Turn the pan upside-down on a serving board. Tap the edges, and let the cake come loose. Frost all sides and serve with cherries on top of the cake.

FUDGED CAKE

This gooey, fudgy cake will have you sneaking bites behind your roommate's back. This recipe is fantastic for parties or special occasions. The time required may seem daunting, but don't worry. It is a simple process you do over a couple hours to allow the cake to cool.—Chelsea

Makes 15 pieces | Time: about 2 hours

1 box chocolate cake mix
necessary ingredients for cake mix (normally oil and eggs)
1 (14.5-oz.) can sweetened condensed milk
⅓ cup semi-sweet chocolate chips
1 (8-oz.) pkg. or container whipped cream
2 sections (1.55-oz) Hershey bar

1. Make cake according to directions on box.
2. Once cake is baked, allow to cool for 30–40 minutes.
3. Dip the round handle of a spatula in water and make 5–6 rows of holes in cake. Redip spatula bottom in water for each hole.
4. Add sweetened condensed milk and ⅓ chocolate chips to a small pot on medium heat. Stir continuously until chocolate is melted. Immediately remove from heat and evenly pour over cake.
5. Allow cake to cool in the fridge for another 20 minutes then frost with whip cream. Grate Hershey bar over the cake for the finishing touch.

(with gluten-free cake mix)

ICE CREAM CHOCOLATE MOUND CAKE

This cake should be illegal with the amount of sugary goodness trapped inside it. It is perfect for big parties and chocolate ice cream lovers.—Chelsea

Makes 12–15 servings
Time: 4–5 hours (including freezing)
For best results, make the day before you need it

2 boxes brownie mix with corresponding ingredients
2 half gallons different ice cream (peanut butter cup, snickers, chocolate, vanilla, etc.)
¾ (8-oz.) container whipped cream
¼ cup heath bits

1. Follow directions on the brownie boxes and bake on a large cookie sheet for about 30–40 minutes or until knife inserted in the middle of the pan comes up clean.

2. Allow brownies to cool. Once cooled, evenly smash brownies on the inside of a large-sized bowl. (There may be a bit of brownies left over. Just eat those.)

3. Pull ice cream out of the freezer and allow to thaw for about 10 minutes. Fill bowl with ice cream. Cover bowl and freeze.

4. After at least 4 hours, remove bowl from freezer. If ice cream melted down below brownie line, use a butter knife to fold brownie down so the brownie and ice cream are even. Then allow bowl to float in hot water in the sink for 3–5 minutes. Quickly flip bowl over onto a cookie sheet. Bowl should slip right off and leave a massive

brownie mound. Cover with whipped cream and sprinkle with Heath bits. Then slice away!

To refreeze, place on a plate and cover with tinfoil.

(with gluten-free brownie
mix and ice cream)

PEANUT BUTTER CHOCOLATE CHIP COOKIES

These flourless bites of bliss will have your sugar and chocolate craving cured in no time!—Chelsea

Makes about 15 cookies | Time: 20 minutes

1 cup peanut butter
1 cup brown sugar
1 egg
½ tsp. baking soda
½ cup chocolate chips

1. Preheat oven to 350 degrees.
2. Mix all ingredients together in a bowl.
3. Lightly oil or butter cookie sheet. Then scoop cookie dough onto sheet with a small spoon. Use a fork to press down on cookie one way and then the other to make a criss-cross pattern.
4. Bake for 8–10 minutes.
5. Allow cookies to cool for several minutes and then enjoy!

(without chocolate)

SUGAR COOKIES

The cream cheese in these cookies gives them a melt-in-your-mouth taste and softness. They're some of the best cookies you can give new neighbors or anyone you want to impress.—Ashley

Makes 2–3 dozen cookies, depending on size
Time: 30 minutes

1 cup unsalted butter
1 cup sugar
1 large egg
2 oz. cream cheese (do not use fat-free)
½ tsp. vanilla
½ tsp. almond extract
1 tsp. lemon zest
3 cups flour
1½ tsp. baking powder
½ tsp. salt

Frosting
3 cups powdered sugar
3–4 Tbsp. milk
2 Tbsp. light corn syrup
¾ tsp. almond extract
food coloring

sprinkles, colored sugar, etc.

1. In a large mixing bowl, cream together butter and sugar using a mixer on medium speed until light and fluffy. Scrape the edges of the bowl and add egg, beating until well-incorporated, about 30 seconds. Add cream cheese and beat for 1 minute. Scrape down the bowl once

more, and add vanilla, almond extract, and lemon zest, beating until incorporated.

2. In a separate bowl, whisk together flour, baking powder, and salt. Keeping the mixer on low, slowly add the dry ingredients to the butter mixture, mixing until just incorporated and dough has formed.

3. Preheat oven to 350 degrees. Divide dough into fourths. Roll each fourth out to ¼-inch thickness on a floured surface or parchment paper. Don't roll any thinner or the cookies will get hard. Cut the dough into desired shapes with cookie cutters and set on a baking sheet.

4. Bake for 9–11 minutes or until the cookies are just barely golden brown. Let cool completely.

5. To make the frosting, beat all ingredients but food coloring together until incorporated. Add food coloring as desired and continue beating for about 1 minute. Spread on cookies and top with sprinkles, nonpareils, colored sugar, or whatever you like.

SHORTBREAD

Shortbread, with its short ingredient list and simple execution, is one of the easiest desserts I know! You can serve it plain, or dress it up to make it a fancier dessert. Shortbread can also be used as a crust in other desserts that adds a buttery sweetness to a creamy topping.—Ashley

Makes 20 servings | Time: 30 minutes

¾ cup sugar
3 cups flour
1 pinch salt
2 sticks butter (16 Tbsp.), cubed

COOKING TIP:
To cube the butter, get a square cleaver if you have one. Cut the butter in half lengthwise, and then turn both pieces to cut again. Stack them back together, and cut into fourths widthwise.

1. Preheat oven to 350 degrees.
2. Combine all ingredients with your bare hands or with a pastry cutter, until the butter is completely blended into the dry ingredients. It should hold its shape to an extent.
3. Press mixture into an 8 x 8 dish, extending out to the corners until you have formed a firm, smooth layer. Puncture the mixture in neat rows with a fork. Bake for about 20 minutes, or until just golden brown. Let cool.
4. Slice into rectangle cookies and serve.

Variations: Melt Kraft caramels with water and spread over the top. Let cool. Melt dark chocolate chips and spread over the caramel. As the chocolate is cooling, sprinkle with just a bit of sea salt.

Cherry shortbread
1 tsp. vanilla
½ tsp. almond extract
1 Tbsp. maraschino cherry juice
about 16 maraschino cherries, chopped
about 1½ cups semi-sweet chocolate chips
chocolate chips, dark or white, melted

> **HEALTH TIP:**
> Need to make it dairy-free? Substitute lard or shortening, or for a low-fat option, try solid (room temperature or colder) coconut oil.

1. Combine vanilla, almond extract, and juice with the mixture above. When the dough has become very soft, mix in chopped cherries and chocolate chips. Drizzle with melted chocolate after baking and cutting into rectangles.

CAKE BALLS

Popular at parties, and very easy to make! This is an excellent way to use leftover cake if you don't have the time to make a cake from a box. But if you do have the time to make a cake, the recipe makes a huge amount of treats for any crowd.

Make sure to match types of chocolate for the chips and the almond bark!—Ashley

Makes about 48 cake balls | Time: 1 hour

1 box cake mix
½ can frosting
6 oz. chocolate chips
2 blocks almond bark

1. Bake the cake according to directions on the box. When done, let cool completely.

2. Using your hands, crumble the cake to a fine crumb texture in a large bowl. Mix in the frosting until the cake has reached a sticky consistency. Take out small portions (the size of a cookie dough scoop, if you have one), and roll into balls about 1–1½ inches in diameter.

3. Melt the chocolate chips and almond bark in a microwave-safe bowl in 30-second intervals, stirring between each. Dip each ball into the chocolate, and coat entirely. Using two spoons, scoop out the ball and allow excess chocolate to drip off. Let slide carefully off spoon onto a baking sheet to dry.

4. While the cake balls are still wet, top with nonpareils or sprinkles. Serve once dry.

Some great flavor combinations: strawberry or

raspberry and chocolate; spice cake and white chocolate with cinnamon frosting; red velvet with cream cheese frosting and chocolate.

OREO TRUFFLES

Similar to cake balls, these are a good way to use up cookies like Oreos. They're darker and richer than most cake balls, but aren't so heavy that you can't eat as many as you like at a time.—Ashley

Makes about 42 truffles | Time: 30 minutes

1 (20-oz.) package Oreos
1 (8-oz.) package cream cheese
2 (12-oz.) packages white chocolate chips

Directions

1. Crush 8–9 Oreos in a bag with a rolling pin until they have become fine crumbs. Set aside for later use.

2. Crush remaining Oreos and put in a medium bowl. Add cream cheese and mix until well combined. Take out small portions, and roll into balls about 1 inch in diameter.

3. Melt chocolate chips in a microwave-safe bowl in 30-second intervals, stirring between each. Dip each ball into the chocolate, coating entirely. Using two spoons, scoop out the ball and allow excess chocolate to drip off. Let slide carefully off spoon onto a baking sheet to dry.

4. While the truffles are still wet, top with the remaining Oreo crumbs. Serve once dry.

CARAMEL ROLLS

These should not be as easy to make for how addicting they can be. Always serve warm so that the caramel is nice and gooey. They cool fast if not eaten immediately, but they reheat all right.—Ashley

Makes 24 rolls | Time: 20 minutes

1 (8-oz.) tube crescent dough
24 square caramels, unwrapped
1 cup sugar
4 Tbsp. cinnamon

1. Preheat oven to 350 degrees. Unroll the dough carefully on wax paper. Cut each triangle in half, and wrap around each of the caramels, forming a ball. Make sure there are no holes in the dough for the caramel to leak through.

2. Combine the sugar and cinnamon in a bowl. Adjust if necessary. Roll each ball in cinnamon sugar mixture. Place about 1 inch apart on a baking sheet.

3. Bake for about 12 minutes, or until golden brown and puffy. Remove from oven, and serve warm.

BETTER THAN A SCHOLARSHIP BROWNIES

I love English toffee crumbled over these brownies, but you can pick any kind of candy you like to give it that final kick of flavor or crunch. If you are planning to eat it all at once, spread with whipped topping before slicing and serving. Otherwise, top each individual serving so that it will keep better.—Ashley

Makes 12 brownies | Time: 50 minutes

1 box brownie mix (the fudgier the better)
½ cup sweetened condensed milk
½ cup caramel ice cream topping
whipped topping
candy of your choice, chopped or crumbled into small
pieces

1. Make brownie mix according to directions on the box. When a toothpick inserted into the middle of the brownie comes out with crumbs but no batter, let cool completely. Only after it's completely cool, evenly poke holes in brownies with a fork.

2. Combine sweetened condensed milk and caramel. Pour over brownies, and allow to soak in.

3. Slice up brownies and top each portion with whipped cream and candy to serve.

CANDY BROWNIES

For some people, finishing off candy from a holiday or a party can be hard to do after a while. There's often so much of it, and it's only possible to eat a lot for so long. For other people, this is just a great new twist on brownies.

If you're a bit sugared out, try using Healthier Brownies (following page), or make the brownies from scratch with reduced fat and sugar, or else the richness of the brownie may get a little overwhelming.—Ashley

Makes 12 | Time: 30 minutes

1 box brownie mix
coconut oil
candy of your choice
chocolate chips, optional
nuts, optional (peanuts, pecans, almonds)

1. Preheat oven to 350 degrees, or according to the brownie mix box. Lightly grease a 9 x 13 baking dish. Make the brownie mix according to directions on the box; however, replace butter with coconut oil.

2. Pour half of the brownie mix into the baking dish, spreading evenly. Set candy of choice throughout the mix, along with chips and nuts if using, and then pour the remaining brownie mix on top.

3. Bake for about 30 minutes or until a toothpick inserted into the middle of the brownies comes out with crumbs but no batter. Cool before cutting into squares.

HEALTHIER BROWNIES

This is a great way to make brownies from scratch to reduce fat and sugar! These brownies are still delicious and chocolatey, without the regret.—Ashley

1¼ cups chocolate chips
½ cup coconut oil
¾ cup unsweetened cocoa powder
½ cup sugar
¼ cup brown sugar
1 tsp. vanilla extract
3 eggs
½ tsp. salt
1 cup flour

1. Preheat oven to 350 degrees and lightly grease a 9 x 13 baking dish.
2. Melt chocolate chips and coconut oil in the microwave in 30-second bursts, stirring after each one. In a large bowl, mix chocolate and cocoa powder until well combined. Add sugars and vanilla extract, stirring to combine. Stir in eggs one at a time until well combined, and add salt. Gently stir in flour until just combined and no lumps are visible.
3. Pour the brownie mix into the baking dish, spreading evenly. Bake for about 30 minutes or until a toothpick inserted into the middle of the brownies comes out with crumbs but no batter. Cool before cutting into squares.

LEMON CREAM CHEESECAKE BARS

My aunt makes these, and they are a favorite for her whole family! They make a great dessert, and can be easily altered for whatever flavor combination you like.

Makes about 24 bars | Time: 25 minutes

1 (3-oz.) package dry lemon Jell-O mix
1 (8-oz.) pkg. cream cheese
1 pinch salt
1 Tbsp. lemon juice
1 cup sugar
1 tsp. vanilla
1 pint whipped cream

Crust
¼ cup butter, melted
about 21 graham crackers, crushed

1. Dissolve Jell-O in boiling water according to package directions. Set until it has formed a syrup.

2. In a bowl, mix cream cheese, salt, lemon juice, sugar, and vanilla. Add the whipped cream to the Jell-O. Mix the cream cheese and Jell-O mixtures together. Set aside to cool completely.

3. To make the crust, preheat oven to 400 degrees. Stir butter and graham crackers together and press in the bottom of a lightly greased 9 x 13 baking pan. Bake for a few minutes in the oven to set.

4. Pour cream cheese mixture evenly into crust and spread with a spatula to smooth. Sprinkle with any

leftover crushed graham crackers. Store in refrigerator overnight to set up.

Variations: Use chocolate graham crackers and orange Jell-O instead for a Halloween or fall twist, or fresh raspberries and raspberry-flavored Jell-O for summer.

(EASY)

LEMON BARS

I like strong lemon flavor, so I've added quite a bit to this recipe. You can add more or less to taste.—Ashley

Makes about 24 | Time: 50 minutes

1 recipe Shortbread Dough (page 209)
6 large eggs
3 cups sugar
2 Tbsp. lemon zest
1½ cups lemon juice
1 cup flour
powdered sugar
blueberries, optional

1. Preheat oven to 350 degrees. Lightly grease a 9 x 13 pan.
2. Press shortbread dough into the base of the pan to form a crust. Bake for about 15 minutes. Let cool.
3. Beat eggs, sugar, lemon zest, lemon juice, and flour in a large bowl until fluffy and creamy. Pour over crust and use a spatula to spread evenly to the corners.
4. Bake for another 30 minutes or so until filling has set. Cool to room temperature or chill overnight if making ahead.
5. Dust all over with powdered sugar and fresh blueberries immediately before serving.

Variation: If you prefer a graham cracker crust, refer to the crust on page 218 (Lemon Cream Cheesecake Bars) and press that into the bottom of the pan instead of the shortbread.

BAKLAVA

I know this recipe doesn't sound like something you can make in college, but I am serious when I say you can! Though the flaky, honey-soaked layers look like a challenge, there are some shortcuts you can take to make this impressive dessert.—Ashley

Makes about 18 | Time: 1 hour 5 minutes

1½ cup chopped pecans or walnuts
1 tsp. cinnamon
1 (16-oz.) package phyllo dough
1 cup butter, partially melted
1 cup water
1 cup sugar
1 tsp. vanilla
½ cup honey

1. Preheat oven to 350 degrees. Butter a 9 x 13 baking dish.
2. Toss nuts and cinnamon in a small bowl. Set aside. Unroll phyllo dough. If necessary, cut in half to fit the pan. Keep covered with a dampened, clean cloth; otherwise, it will dry out and become unusable. Make sure the cloth is not too wet, or the dough will become soggy.
3. Layer the baklava as follows: Place two sheets of dough in the pan. Brush thoroughly with butter, making sure to cover the edges. Repeat four times so that the dough is eight sheets thick. Sprinkle with a couple tablespoons of nut mixture, and top with two sheets of dough and butter. Repeat until you have about 6–8 sheets of dough left. Layer the remaining sheets as in the first step (two sheets brushed with butter) until done.
4. Using a sharp knife, slice down through the layers

and cut diagonally to form triangle shapes. Bake for 50 minutes or until baklava is golden brown and crisp.

5. While baklava is baking, boil water and sugar until sugar is melted. Add vanilla and honey. Simmer for about 20 minutes.

6. Remove baklava, and immediately pour sauce over it. Let cool, and serve.

CREAM CHEESE STUFFED STRAWBERRIES

Filling strawberries with a creamy mixture is a great way to dress up fresh, delicious fruit. These will become irresistible, especially when strawberries are delicious and ripe in the spring!—Ashley

Makes 24 servings | Time: 1 hour 10 minutes

2 dozen large strawberries
1 (8-oz.) package cream cheese, softened
½ cup powdered sugar
1 tsp. vanilla

1. Cut stems off strawberries and set tip up on a cutting board. Slice an X downward into the strawberry. Do not cut all the way through. Set aside.

2. Mix cream cheese, sugar, and vanilla with a hand mixer until fluffy. Fill a plastic bag with the mixture. If you have a frosting tip, fix this to the bag; otherwise, just cut off the corner. Squeeze the mixture into each of the strawberries.

3. Chill for at least 1 hour and serve.

STICKY MANGO RICE

Warm and sweet with little effort, this Thai dessert goes fantastically with curries and Pad Thai. It eases the spice of some of these dishes, but is no less flavorful or delightful.

The best rice to use here is sticky and/or sweet rice, like sushi or jasmine rice. It's a good way to use leftover white rice, if it can be reheated to hold its shape.—Ashley

Makes 8 servings | Time: 10 minutes

1 (13-oz.) can coconut milk
½ cup sugar
¼ tsp. salt
4 cups cooked rice, sticky
2–3 mangoes, sliced

1. Combine coconut cream, sugar, and salt in a medium saucepan over medium heat until sugar dissolves. Reserve ½ cup for topping.

2. Remove from heat and stir in rice. Serve about ½ cup per serving. Top with mangoes and 1–2 tablespoons cream topping.

I-CAN'T-BELIEVE-IT'S-GOAT-CHEESE TARTS

At first bite, I couldn't believe these mini cheesecakes didn't taste like the strong goat cheese I'd become familiar with. Even roommates who dislike goat cheese couldn't get enough of these tarts! I also couldn't believe how much easier they were than regular cheesecake, which requires a springform pan.—Ashley

Makes 10 servings | Time: 30 minutes

Crust

1 cup graham cracker crumbs

½ cup sugar

½ cup coconut oil, melted

Filling

8 oz. goat cheese, beaten

2 eggs

½ cup sugar

2 cups sliced strawberries

½ cup chocolate chips, melted

small mint leaves, optional

fresh whipped cream, optional

1. Crust: Fill a muffin or cupcake tin with liners. Mix ingredients together and press into the liners.

2. Filling: Beat cheese, eggs, and sugar together until smooth. Pour into liners over crust. Bake at 325 degrees for 20 minutes.

3. Let cool, and top with fresh berries. Drizzle melted chocolate over the tarts, and garnish with mint leaves and a tiny dollop of whipped cream if desired.

Variation: Replace graham cracker crumbs with Oreo crumbs, and strawberries with whole raspberries for a chocolatey rich treat.

(with gluten-free
cookies or cracker)

DRINK UP!

STRAWBERRY BASIL LEMONADE

Making your own lemonade allows you to control the sugars and preservatives in a drink. Also, you have the added benefit of knowing exactly how much lemon juice is in your lemonade!—Ashley

Makes 6–8 servings | Time: 2 minutes

juice of 3 lemons
2 large (at least 2 inches) strawberries
6 cups cold water
¾ cup sugar
1 tsp. dried basil, OR 3 large fresh leaves, julienned

In a large pitcher, combine all ingredients and store in refrigerator for about 30 minutes, or up to a week.

GINGER TEA

Feeling awful during cold season? Need to sing in public and your voice needs some TLC? Just love the taste of tea? The healing combination of ginger, herbs, and lemon is great for all of the above!

For making your own blends or using loose leaf blends, make sure that you have a diffuser to keep your tea from becoming a mess. I got a diffuser mug for not very much that has a removable porcelain filter and a lid to keep the steam in.—Ashley

Makes 1 servings | Time: 10 minutes

½ Tbsp. grated ginger
2–3 large basil leaves OR 2 tsp. dried rosemary
1 Tbsp. lemon juice
dash apple cider vinegar
1 tsp. honey

1. Bring water to a boil in a kettle if you have one, or in a microwave safe cup if you do not.
2. Place ginger and herbs in diffuser in a teacup or mug, and pour boiling water over it into the cup. Add lemon juice, apple cider vinegar, and honey. Cover and let steep for about 5 minutes. Drink warm.

UNIQUE INGREDIENT INDEX

7. Almond Milk

a. Peanut Butter Banana Shake 27

b. Fruit Breakfast Shake 30

c. Creamy Banana Apple Oatmeal 31

d. Monte Cristo Sandwiches 41

e. Roasted Veggie and Chicken Chowder 80

f. Chicken Cordon Bleu Casserole 134

8. Beef bouillon

a. Lasagna Soup 86

b. Homemade Tomato Soup 112

9. Galangal

a. Tom Kha Gai 92

10. Ginger

a. Chicken Spring Rolls and Peanut Sauce 59

b. Tom Kha Gai 92

c. Mongolian Beef 155

d. Thai Chicken Tacos 163

e. Carne Asada Torta 175

f. Ginger Tea 229

11. Sriracha

a. Onigiri (Spicy Tuna Roll) 55

b. Mango Cilantro Dipping Sauce 57

18. Sun-dried tomatoes

19. Pesto

20. Tomato paste

21. Hoisin sauce

Acknowledgments

I owe every ounce of sanity I was able to maintain during these long hours slaving in the kitchen to my angel husband, William Jackson. I'm not the only one who can cook in our house! I don't think I will ever make chicken as tender as he does. I also wanted to thank family and friends for their encouragement and assistance! I've also had a wonderful coauthor and Cedar Fort team that have helped make this crazy project possible. Thank you everyone!
—Chelsea

I would never have learned to cook without my mom, who pulled me away from my very interesting books to help her prepare dinner. Because of her, I managed to survive college without overdosing on stovetop ramen. Thank you to the best chef I know! I also want to thank my roommates, Hannah and Kim, who played guinea pig to my recipes for months. Thank you to Chelsea, who has been an amazing coauthor for me, and to Cedar Fort for helping me make this book a reality!
—Ashley

About A. N. Gephart

Hearty and complex foods were always a huge part of **ASHLEY N. GEPHART**'s life. The love of eating miraculously carried her through Utah Valley University without starving, and only increased once she landed a job as a cookbook editor. Now she perfects recipes, scours the Internet for tantalizing food photography, and tests out her finds on her friends. Aside from experimenting with almost any recipe she can find, she enjoys history, design, playing hammy roles on the stage, and contemplating what it would be like to be a supervillain. She lives in her native Utah.

About Chelsea Jackson

CHELSEA JACKSON graduated from Brigham Young University with a major in English and a minor in editing but admits that "lunch time" is still her favorite subject. She grew up with an incredible mother who could make anything taste delicious—and still make it healthy. Thanks to a doctor as a father, a mother as a health and wellness coach, AND surviving college, Chelsea knows tips and tricks for eating fun and healthy food as a college student. Chelsea now enjoys concocting gluten-free recipes for her best friend and husband, who has celiac disease.

My Additional Recipes

My Additional Recipes